## THE *THINKING CLEARLY* SERIES
*Series editor: Clive Calver*

The *Thinking Clearly* series sets out the main issues in a variety of important subjects. Written from a mainstream Christian stand-point, the series combines clear biblical teaching with up-to-date scholarship. Each of the contributors is an authority in his or her field. The series is written in straightforward everyday language, and each volume includes a range of practical applications and guidance for further reading.

The series has two main aims:
1. To help Christians understand their faith better.
2. To show how Christian truths can illuminate matters of crucial importance in our society.

"In a book that ranges from near-death experiences, to hell, via a consideration of reincarnation, immortality, bodily resurrection, purgatory, and heaven, Dr Twelftree brings clarity to an often confusing and involved area of debate.

"Dr Twelftree asks important questions and examines the evidence for life after death within the major faith settings, before concentrating upon the Christian evidence and experience. Writing in an accessible and informed manner, he builds his argument through successive chapters, giving clear consideration of all points of view.

"The title of this book is not misleading. Graham Twelftree approaches his subject with honesty and has the ability to ask questions that both inform and stimulate our thinking, bringing clarity to the subject.

"This is a valuable introduction to the debate concerning life after death."

– Canon Dr Christina Baxter, Principal,
St John's College, Nottingham

"The theme of this book is relevant to EVERYONE. It is an engaging and sound guide. Read it before you die."

– J. John, author and evangelist

"This is quite simply the most outstanding book in its field and is certain to become the definitive study of what the Bible says about life after death. Every Christian should have a copy, and every preacher should teach the material contained within these pages: they contain a wealth of truth and hope. I congratulate Dr Twelftree on a wonderful achievement and highly recommend his book. It should be read by everyone, including those who do not yet go to church."

– Rev. Dr Mark Stibbe, author, theologian and
Vicar of St Andrew's, Chorleywood

THE *THINKING CLEARLY* SERIES

*Series editor: Clive Calver*

# *Life After Death*

## GRAHAM H. TWELFTREE

MONARCH
BOOKS

Mill Hill, London & Grand Rapids, Michigan

First published by Monarch Books in the UK 2002,
Concorde House, Grenville Place,
Mill Hill, London, NW7 3SA.

Published in the USA by Monarch Books 2002.

Distributed by:
UK: STL, PO Box 300, Kingstown Broadway, Carlisle,
Cumbria CA3 0QS;
USA: Kregel Publications, PO Box 2607
Grand Rapids, Michigan 49501.

ISBN 1 85424 525 2

**British Library Cataloguing Data**
A catalogue record for this book is available
from the British Library.

Book design and production for the publishers by
Bookprint Creative Services
P.O. Box 827, BN21 3YJ, England
Printed in Great Britain.

# Contents

To the people of Lameroo
and to the memory of John Pocock (1921–1999)

# Preface

George Bernard Shaw famously quipped that the only certain statistic is the 100% death rate. No matter how long we live, or how we fill our lives, we all face the inevitable trauma and finality of death – perhaps sooner than we imagine.

We probably all share the most pressing questions about death: Is death the end? If there is an after-life, what is it going to be like? Will we be absorbed into a spiritual realm? Or, will we be conscious of some distinct personal existence? If we have a soul, is that what lives on after this life? Or, will we have some kind of body in the next life?

Some readers will be asking what we are to make of the ideas of reincarnation, of purgatory, limbo and the intermediate state. And, should we pray for the dead? Many readers will be asking about heaven and hell: What are they like and who goes where? On hell the fundamental issue is likely to be: Can a good God send people to hell? The most frequently asked questions about heaven are probably: Where is it? What will we do for ever? Will we know our relatives and friends in heaven?

We may never know the answers to these questions with the certainty some crave. However, through this book I hope readers' thinking will become clearer about the possibilities and also understand the Christian expectation that death is not the end – at least for those who die in Christ.

We will, however, be left with two of the most important questions faced by human beings: How can we live if we are going to die, and how can we die if we are going to live for ever? Therefore, in the last chapter we will be suggesting some practical answers to these two key questions.

While I have written this book to help readers think clearly about life after death, there is much that I will not be covering. For example, I will not be dealing specifically with death and dying. Also, there has not been space for an extended treatment of the resurrection of Jesus, so foundational for arguing for life after death. Nor will I be dealing in any direct way with the so-called end times or the second coming of Jesus. That is the subject of another book in this series.

Even though I will be seeking insights from the sciences, the philosophy of religion, psychology, and even parapsychology, these fields will not be the main focus of our study. In this book I will be taking a particular kind of approach that gives pride of place to the Bible in shaping Christian thinking and in sifting through the possibilities concerning the after-life. I want to help readers who take the Bible to be the most important source for forming religious views to think clearly about life after death.

If the Bible is important in forming your views you will probably assume that what follows will confirm your views. I cannot promise such a comfortable journey. Thinking clearly with the Bible open can turn up some challenging conclusions. Should you become disturbed by some of my conclusions, I only ask that you consider whether or not I have been faithful to the message of the various passages in the Bible.

Using so few endnotes has hidden from view most of my scholarly creditors. Even the small section on further reading at the back of the book is little more than a part payment of my large and readily acknowledged debts.

Once again, the staff members of Luther Seminary library, Adelaide, are to be applauded for their ongoing help in providing kind and generous support for my research. Thank you. Also, thank you to those who have read earlier drafts of this book: Rodger Bassham, Wayne Donald, Arthur Jackson, Jeff Mountford, Philip Muston, Susan Robertson and Brenton Wait. They must take considerable credit for helping me remove errors and sharpening my thinking. It is a particular honour to have had Arthur Jackson (still going strong in his 80s) read and comment on a rough draft of this book for, like the great Saint Basil (330–379), he brought to the reading his passion to hold together pastoral concerns and scholarly precision.

Graham H. Twelftree
Regent University, Virginia, USA, 2002

# 1

## Is Death the End?

With the knowledge that one day we will die often comes the fear of death. Yet hope springs eternal! I will be arguing that our hope of life after death is reasonable. This is because of the probable existence of God to make this possible and also because we can argue that we are inherently immortal. We can even speak of the need for life after death to give the opportunity for the injustices of the world to be put right the other side of death. One of the most compelling hints that we can be confident in living beyond the grave are the reports of near-death experiences.

# Is Death the End?

"When the dust drinks up a man's blood,
Once he is slain, there is no return to life"
Aeschylus

"Hope springs eternal in the human breast"
Alexander Pope

From the knowledge of our death arises an almost universal fear. As long ago as before 700 BC, Homer, the ancient Greek narrative poet, made the quip that he would rather be a live slave than a dead king (*Odyssey* 11:487). In our time, Woody Allen made the wisecrack: "I'm not afraid to die; I just don't want to be there when it happens." Not surprisingly he also said, "I don't want to achieve immortality through my work. I want to achieve immortality through not dying."

## An almost universal fear?

In his *Confessions*, the British broadcaster–philosopher Bryan Magee says that in mid-life the realization hit him like a demolition crane that he was inevitably going to die. It was for him a nightmare, a feeling of being trapped and unable to escape from his death – the inevitability of his literal and total destruction.[1]

The terror of death intensifies as we realize that it separates us from those we love and the things we have acquired and enjoyed during our lives. Yet, by the end of this book I hope readers will be able to share the attitude of Dietrich Bonhoeffer (1906–45). His last recorded words to a fellow

12

prisoner before being executed by the Nazis were, "This is the end – for me the beginning of life."[2]

But is hope for life after death a reasonable expectation? Perhaps a belief in an after-life is only a way of consoling ourselves over unfulfilled dreams, or of coping with promising lives cut short by death. The greatest British philosopher of the 20th century, Bertrand Russell (1872–1970), said that it is not rational arguments, but emotions – the fear of death and the value we place on people, for example – that cause belief in a future life.[3] Exploring these issues is the purpose of this introductory chapter.

## Is death the end?

So important is this question that from tribal animism to the highly developed religions of the present day – Hinduism and Christianity, for example – the after-life is a central element of belief systems. In his postscript to his Gifford Lectures delivered at Edinburgh in 1901–02 William James, the Harvard psychologist, put the point bluntly: "Religion . . . for the great majority of our own race *means* immortality, and nothing else. God is the producer of immortality; and whoever has doubts about immortality is written down as an atheist without farther trial."[4]

However, from one perspective, nothing is less probable than life after death. A cold and lifeless body is all the evidence we need that there can be nothing beyond the grave. With the unknown Hebrew poet or poets who gave us the Old Testament book of Job we can ask:

> There is hope for a tree,
> if it is cut down, that it will sprout again . . .
> But mortals die, and are laid low;
> humans expire, and where are they? (Job 14:7, 10).

Some readers may be quick to say that the question of life after death is easily settled by the Bible. However, the Bible is increasingly ignored as a source of religious belief, not only by secular people but also by Christians; and other religions have different ways of establishing belief. Also, even if the Bible does teach or assume belief in life beyond the grave, in order to develop views that are as credible as possible for 21st century people it is important that we discuss not only the credibility of the biblical view of life after death but also what can be established about life after death from other perspectives. In any case, those who take the Bible seriously in guiding belief, or those who want to believe only what the Bible says, may be a little disappointed, for the Bible does not say as much as some readers may hope about life after death.

## Is there life after death?

This most fundamental question is not as straightforward as it first appears.

First, some people claim that the desire for personal survival beyond death is selfish or self-centred. That is, the desire to live beyond death is basically irreligious or ungodly: we ought not to be concerned about our living beyond death. But few will find this view satisfactory. In any case, as we will see in this study, belief in life after death is not based on human longings but arises out of the nature and activity of God. In the next chapter I will argue that God has created us in his image, and that his love can be expected to hold us in existence beyond the grave. Thus, our personal concerns about life after death are not only legitimate but natural and even necessary in the light of God being our Creator and the one who sustains our life.

Secondly, Professor Nicholas Lash, a Roman Catholic theologian of Cambridge, says that any conjecture about what happens beyond the boundary of death is speculation. Citing the Bible – where Paul insists that "no eye has seen, nor ear heard, nor the human heart conceived" what God has in store "for those who love him" (1 Corinthians 2:9) – Lash says we have no idea what happens beyond the grave.[5] He argues that even the imagery of the Bible that relates to our theme points to our present experience, not to the future. If we are to exclude reports such as near-death experiences (see below), Lash is right – at least in part: we have no idea what happens beyond the boundary of death. However, as we will see through this book, our speculations can be more than reasonable. Also, the imagery of the Bible, while having implications for our present experience, does attempt to tell us of something about life beyond the grave.

Thirdly, for some people, whether or not there is life beyond the grave depends on what we mean by "life" or "living". This is not mere hair-splitting. If life after death means we go on having a distinct personal life with a body, then some would say we cannot believe in life after death. But if by life after death we mean that we live on in the thoughts of others or in the life of our children and grandchildren, then we should believe in life after death.

This minimalist view was expressed in 1867 by the novelist George Eliot (1819–80) in the opening lines of her most famous poem:

> Oh may I join the choir invisible
> Of those immortal dead who live again
> In minds made better by their presence.

But this is not very satisfying; in any meaningful sense I no longer exist. There are many from the past who are held in the memory of the living: Socrates, William Shakespeare, Wolfgang Amadeus Mozart, Abraham Lincoln and William Gladstone. From more recent times, Albert Schweitzer, Mother Teresa, and Yehudi Menuhin remain in our memories.

Even if we should multiply this list by a hundred- or a thousandfold, it would still be a mere drop in the vast ocean of people who have lived and died and, after a generation or two, are forgotten as if they had never lived. Clearly, if life after death means to live on in the memory of those who remain, it lacks meaningful content and – importantly – has no impact on the consciousness of those who have died.

An important variation of this view is that life after death means we live on in the memory of God. This view is associated particularly with Charles Hartshorne (1897–2000). That is, our individual lives continue after death in God's memory by his perpetually remembering us. However, in neither of these variations of the "memory" options do we continue to live after death as conscious, acting individuals. These views about life after death are meaningless and can be left aside for more robust views of what it would mean "to live" beyond the rotting tomb.

Having taken these three points into account, we can turn directly to the question as to whether or not there is life after death.

## No! There is no life after death

There are a number of arguments that come to the same point: there is no life after death.

### Death is the end

According to a materialist (for whom there is no reality beyond the "stuff" of this world and life) or a humanist (for whom God plays no part in our affairs), the idea of life beyond death is to be rejected. It is nonsense.

Likewise, the very cornerstone of Buddhism is the rejection of the idea of a substance-like entity in us that will survive death. Whether that substance be called our "self" or a "person" or "being" or "life principle", it is an illusion and certainly not immortal. Even the well-known notion of rebirth or reincarnation, it is said, *must* be interpreted in a way that avoids implying that it is "me" or my "self" which is reborn. Instead, one way of interpreting the Buddhist view of rebirth is to see it as our craving to live on and to see our happiness endure in others after we die. With no after-life the Buddhist is then forced to face death in life. "Die and become thoroughly dead while living and all will be well thereafter", goes the Zen saying.[6]

A similar view was proposed by the German theologian Paul Tillich (1896–1965). In a sermon, "The Eternal Now", he begins by saying that, "It is our destiny and the destiny of everything in our world that we must come to an end." He maintained that any hope for "life after death" or a "world without end" was "foolish, wishful thinking'. In Tillich's view there is no personal survival, even though we may use images taken from time to speak of the eternal. Riddle though this may be for us, the only future we have is the future (that in effect never comes!) which we continually anticipate in the present.[7]

## There is no God to make life after death possible

The life after death assumed in this statement is one in which we are bodily resurrected. At first sight – so the argument goes – the idea of a bodily resurrection seems a simple idea. But, when filled out, it becomes unintelligible. For example, the Canadian atheist Professor Kai Nielson says, "Suppose Sven dies and rots and eventually turns to dust and indeed further suppose his grave gets upturned and the dust, which is all that he is now, is spread randomly by the wind. God, being omnipotent, at the Last Judgement gathers these specks of dust together and reconstitutes them into an energized body."[8]

This, so the argument continues, may be logically possible – as possible as it is for a sprinter to run from Edinburgh to London or from Sydney to Melbourne in a minute – but, without the belief in a God who can do anything, such a bodily resurrection is unintelligible. There being no God, there can be no resurrection of the dead and, therefore, no life after death.

To counter this argument we would have to argue for the existence of a God who could do anything, including raise the dead in this way. While this is not the place to make a full case for the existence of God, we can point to the many coherent and convincing cases that have been made for the existence of God.[9] Thus, if God does exist, as he most probably does, the idea of life after death immediately becomes a distinct possibility, whatever the form of life we can expect to experience.

More importantly for this study, there are ways to think about the resurrection of the body other than to assume that in the Last Judgement God will gather the scattered specks of dust that remain from our dead body and reassemble them (see chapter 5).

*We cannot have a disembodied existence – therefore there is no life after death*

According to this argument, since we can only exist as mind as well as matter – as water only exists as hydrogen and oxygen – there can be no after-life because there can be no disembodied life. Our consciousness or thinking life is so completely dependent on – some would say identical with – a fully functioning, physical brain that when our bodies die we can no longer continue to live in any meaningful sense of the word.

So important for thinking about life after death is this issue of the relationship between our mind and our body that it has been claimed that the only way we can begin to get anywhere in considering life after death is to understand human beings as, in some way, having personalities (or some immaterial substance such as a "soul") independent of our bodies. The fully developed view of what is called dualism, famously defended by the French philosopher René Descartes (1596–1650), is that our real or essential nature is not physical but non-physical. Descartes took this view because, he said, we are conscious of thought and experience, even if that thought and experience is intimately connected with our bodies.

There are such good arguments for "us" to continue to exist without our bodies that we shall be using chapters 4 and 5 to explore aspects of this option.

This review of some of the arguments against after-life has been very brief, for much of this book can be taken as an answer to those who say death is the end. In the next chapter we will see not only that expectations of life after death have a long history but that the origins of Christian views are both interesting and unique. In chapters 3 and 4 we will examine two popular and equally longstanding approaches to the after-life: reincarnation and the immortality of our soul. However, as we will see, these views are neither reasonable nor credible as an expectation for our after-life. We will also argue that these beliefs have no legitimate place in traditional or biblical Christianity. Instead, we will see (chapter 5) that we need to place our hopes for an after-life in some form of the resurrection of our body. To get our case started we will begin with a glimpse at the "yes" case.

## Yes! There is life after death

If we are going to say anything convincing about life after death we need to show that it is more reasonable to think that we survive death than that death marks our end. We can do this in a number of ways.

### We are inherently immortal

We could support the idea of life after death by arguing that we are immortal by nature. (I am using the word "immortal" in its older sense of "living beyond death" rather than in the modern technical sense we will be using it in chapter 4, of living without a body.) Even though writers in the Bible did not use this line of argument that we are "inherently immortal" (see chapter 2), it is now a common argument for life after death. We will say more about this in chapter 4, but a number of preliminary points are in order here to help establish our case for life after death.

First, we could come to the conclusion that we are inherently immortal by considering the great value and unique irreplaceability of every person. For a person (say our best friend) to be annihilated at death would violate all we understand about human dignity; if death was the end, then our whole life would be rendered pointless and empty. If the birth, astounding growth in insight and creativity of every human being was no more than a brief flowering to be obliterated at death, then Shakespeare's character, Macbeth, was right:

> Life's but a walking shadow, a poor player,
> That struts and frets his hour upon the stage,
> And then is heard no more; it is a tale
> Told by an idiot, full of sound and fury,
> Signifying nothing (*Macbeth* 5:5:16).

The pointlessness of life that is ended in death is not changed even when we take into account the creativity that is left behind by a Mozart or a Monet, for we are talking about the intrinsic value of a person, not what he or she may produce.

Secondly, we might come to think that we are naturally immortal by considering the great power the future has over us. For example, we find that our dreams and drives are never fulfilled in this life. We are always thinking ahead and reaching out beyond ourselves to the future and to dreams and ideals we have yet to attain. Indeed, sometimes our dreams seem unattainable in this life. Therefore, we instinctively look to the future for what we are denied in this present life: happiness, health, peace or knowledge. Even though we cannot be sure what our (or the) future will hold, our future-orientated lives are an expression of the famous statement of Friedrich Nietzsche (1844–1900): "Become what you are!"

Thirdly, another way we might come to the conclusion that we are immortal by nature is by noting the times when we experience life as more than just a series of events: one event after another. For example, when listening to music we sometimes grasp the theme of the piece not just as a series of notes or even phrases but as a unity transcending the moment of our listening. Perhaps we can take this as a most meagre clue as to what is meant by eternity. Life is not just timeless but simultaneously a past, a present and a future. Dare we conclude that this process is not attainable in this life? It is towards this future that we human beings seem inherently to strive: to "the whole simultaneous and complete fruition of a life without bounds", to quote Boethius (c. 480–c. 542 AD), the Roman statesman–philosopher.

Fourthly, we might conclude that we are inherently immortal because human beings seem almost always and everywhere to have believed in some form of after-life. We will see this in the next chapter. As reassuring as this point may be, by itself it is not very convincing, because human beings could have been deluding themselves. Nevertheless, taken together with the other points we have been noting, the widespread and longstanding belief that we can expect an after-life could be a reasonable human longing.

As compelling and comforting as these points may be, in themselves, they do not take us very far beyond the merest hint that believing in life after death is reasonable. But at least we have a start in these hints. To go beyond these whispers we have to include other cases to have any reasonable grounds for clear thinking about life after death. That is our task for the remainder of this chapter.

## Morality would be incomplete in this life

This argument that our natural sense of justice points to the necessity of life after death has its origins in the writings of perhaps the most important European philosopher of modern times, the East Prussian philosopher Immanuel Kant (1724–1804). It runs something like this: the highest good that we can imagine would be a life where we were happy and, at the same time, seeing and experiencing justice and goodness being done to and by us and others. Put another way, our sense of right and wrong tells us that only just people are worthy of experiencing happiness.

However, this is not how we see life around us. On the one hand, we find that doing the right thing (say returning a lost purse or wallet) implies we have to forgo happiness (say, spending the money on ourselves). On the other hand, evil and injustice – dishonest business deals, for example – appear to succeed and lead to happiness. Therefore, to complete this argument, if our sense of morality is to be completed and satisfied we have to assume that life extends beyond what we presently know. In short, our natural sense of justice points to the necessity of life after death. Otherwise our sense of justice, for example with regard to a Hitler or a Pol Pot, is delusory.

## Psychical research

We turn now to what is seen to be the most controversial yet probably the most reliable indicator of our survival beyond death. In an interview, the Cambridge philosopher C. D. Broad (1887–1971) said that "If the facts of psychical research are true, they literally change everything."[10] This avenue of research is sometimes called, the "paranormal" or "parapsychology". Those who support the value of the paranormal consider that, if we have minds or spirits that can exist independently of our bodies (and therefore survive the death of our body), it should be possible to show this from experiences of encounters with spirits of the dead.

Interest in psychical research was at its height in the 19th century, leading to the formation of the Society for Psychical Research in London in 1882. At that time, there were a number of individuals involved who became well known: Mrs Piper, Mrs Leonard and Mrs Coombe-Tennant (known as Mrs Willett), for example. These people were thought to be remarkably telepathically sensitive and able to communicate with the "dead". In a trance, the consciousness and voice of these individuals (or mediums) were seemingly replaced by those of someone who had died. In this way the dead person was thought to be able to speak with the living.

Here was thought to be good evidence for life after death. However, since the enthusiasm of the 19th century, in most of the 20th century interest in the scientific value of paranormal research declined. Nevertheless, there has been a recent resurgence of interest in parapsychology, marked, for example, by the launching of *The Paranormal Review* (London) by the Society for Psychical Research in 1997.

However, in the face of ongoing enquiries and investigation, questions remain unanswered and sceptics remain unconvinced. For example, if the question about life after death is answered by a reference to "apparitions", why do not the dead always (or more often) make themselves known to the living? And why do the supposed spirits of the dead give no convincing impression of carrying on an existence of their own between seances? It is reasonable to conclude that the other spirit with whom a person communicates is not an independent personality but parts or aspects of the medium's own mind. Alternatively the other spirit could be a spiritual being – good or evil – independent of human existence. In any case, not least because of the hoaxes, inconsistent methodologies, falsified records and fraudulent claims that have been uncovered, parapsychologists are no nearer than they were 150 years ago in helping us think clearly about life after death.[11]

## Near-death experiences

One aspect of psychical research that is of particular interest are reports of near-death experiences (NDEs). These are reports of those who have been resuscitated after having been clinically dead for a few seconds or up to a few minutes. With reports from those who allege they have experienced journeys to another world, we are at least dealing with something which is widely experienced, and it is argued that such stories provide evidence of life after death.

In 1988, at the age of 77, the heart of British philosopher and atheist A. J. Ayer (1910–89) stopped for four minutes. He was astonished to have a near-death experience. During the experience he said he seemed to encounter a distressingly painful, bright red light. He thought that "the painful red light was a warning that the laws of nature were not working properly." He said that, returning to his body, he was dismayed at the prospect of having to die and perhaps experience the harsh light again. Even though he remained an atheist, Ayer said that his experiences weakened his inflexible attitude towards life after death.[12]

## A personal story

From the age of three I suffered from asthma, not a good thing for a young farmer in a dusty country. However, I got by until one December day in 1967. After I had emptied twelve tonnes of wheat from a truck into the silo in the town of Lameroo in South Australia, a cloud of wheat dust triggered a severe asthma attack.

I was rushed to the hospital by John Pocock, in a small maroon truck. In the hospital an oxygen tube was pushed a little way down my throat. The doctor monitored the pulse in my right arm. The matron held my left arm. I caught a glimpse of staff filing into the room to stand around the bed, quietly watching me. Gradually, the sounds of the hospital and the vehicles on the road outside faded from me. And the pain had become so great and all encompassing that it seemed to be no more. As I reclined on the bed in my dirty grey overalls, I knew that my life was ebbing away and now hung in the balance. I knew that, any moment, my body – tired from too little sleep and now without enough oxygen to sustain life – would soon collapse. But I wasn't frightened. I knew that my life belonged to God and that I was safe. However, I was concerned for my parents. I wanted to send them a last message which I hoped would give them some comfort. Knowing I had little energy left, I thought carefully about what I would say. With what I assumed would be my last words, I said – choosing the present tense deliberately, "Tell my parents I'm all right."

I then felt myself leave my body. I – a white and shiny me – lifted away from my dark and exhausted body. I went up a short and narrow passageway, something like a small lift shaft. I was then at the entrance of a most wonderful place. The sounds that rolled through the place, and now over me, were beautiful. There was lovely sound, but it wasn't music. And the colours! They were neither gold nor white: they were brighter and even more beautiful. Normally, you would say that such an experience would be overwhelming, but it wasn't. It was awesome yet attractive, peaceful and, it seemed, where I belonged.

I had only been there a little while, just a spectator about to look around and take part, when God – I do not know how I knew that – stretched out his right hand over me. I could see only his hand, wrist and forearm as it came into my field of vision over the end of the passageway that opened out just above me. He said to me, "No, Graham, not yet!" He didn't push me. Perhaps he encouraged me. Or did he let me go back? But, in a moment that had no time, I rested back into my body.

The sounds and sensations of the hospital became known to me again. The first thing I heard was the voice of Matron Redaway, who was still holding my left arm. "He's all right now," she said with some relief. I lay there quietly as the staff filed out of the room. I was to stay there for another seven days, for a very slow but complete recovery.

## Near-death experiences: an assessment

When I had that NDE I had no idea that it was relatively common.[13] In 1983, a Gallup poll survey found that 8 million people in the United States claimed to have had such experiences. An editorial in *The Lancet* (London, 24 June 1978, p. 1347) suggested that accounts bear striking similarities:

> Amongst the experiences many have described are an initial period of distress followed by profound calm and joy; out-of-body experiences with the sense of watching resuscitation events from a distance; the sensation of moving rapidly down a tunnel or along a road, accompanied by a loud buzzing or ringing noise or hearing beautiful music; recognising friends and relatives who have died previously; a rapid visual review of pleasant incidents from throughout life as a panoramic play-back (in perhaps 12 per cent of cases); a sense of approaching a border or frontier and being sent back; and being annoyed or disappointed at having to return from such a pleasant experience.

What are we to make of such reports? Answers are not easily found. An important aspect of the thousands of stories – such as those reported from children – is that some of the children have not had time to be influenced by stories adults may have heard or read.

Clearly, in my case, I was not dead – if I had been, I could not have been resuscitated. (By definition, death is just beyond the point from which anyone can return to tell us anything.) Nevertheless, it was a close encounter with death. Was it a dream? Was it the final workings of an overtired or dying mind? Was I experiencing some kind of self-assurance in the face of extinction? Or was I glimpsing the beginning of my life after death?

It could be that the change in blood pressure in my inner ear gave me the sensation of rising. Perhaps as I was dying, there were chemical changes in my brain that led to the experience. But, for example, the view that ketamine and morphine contribute to the experiences cannot be supported, for those not taking these drugs also report having these experiences. It cannot be oxygen deprivation, for that usually leads to a confused state, the opposite to a near-death experience. It cannot be wishful thinking, for the religious and the atheist both tell of deathbed visions and NDEs. It cannot be a malfunctioning of the central nervous system, or fever, or hallucinatory pain-killing drugs or particular psychological states that account for NDEs. If this was the explanation for NDEs, then the reports would be much more common. Only 15% of people who are resuscitated have a story to tell of their experience.[14]

The most popular explanation of NDEs is "depersonalization", the theory that our mind constructs a powerful fantasy to protect ourself against the threat of destruction. However, depersonalization almost never occurs in people over 40, while people of all ages report NDEs. In the end, it is not unreasonable to conclude that those having a near-death experience are catching glimpses of an after-life from "this side". If this is a reasonable conclusion, we have evidence – be it ever so slight – that we have a hint that we can anticipate life beyond the grave. That is, in the words of the philosopher Ronald W. K. Paterson, who has also examined the evidence from psychical research, including near-death experiences: "on the whole, but quite clearly, the facts point in the direction of personal survival of bodily death."[15]

## So far ...

Strictly speaking, we cannot *know* what ultimately happens after we die – whether it is the end or whether, in some way, we continue to experience individual, meaningful life. We have noted that there is some doubt about the veracity of the testimony of those who report having been dead. Indeed, if death is the permanent cessation of life from which no recovery is possible, we cannot say we have accounts of either the possibility or nature of life after death.

However, in looking at the arguments for and against life after death, we have seen that pessimism is unwarranted and unreasonable; there are around us clear intimations of immortality.

- We saw that we are probably inherently immortal: if our experience of this world is really intelligible then there is more than this life.
- From considering the unique value and purpose of individual human life, as well as our innate sense of morality, there is a moral argument to be made for life after death.
- Further, if God exists, as he probably does, he could not only make such a life possible but also be able to involve others in his sphere of life and therefore be the goal of the after-life.
- Also, we have seen that reports of near-death experiences probably offer the best experiential hint of an after-life.

A more complete case for believing in life after death and its likely form are the twin themes of this book. As we enter into the contemporary debates about the various theories of reincarnation, immortality, resurrection, purgatory, limbo, the intermediate state, heaven and hell, judgement, universalism, and conditional immortality, we will be building a case for life after death. We will also be seeing what kind of life we can expect after we die.

Given that death is not the end, there are generally thought to be three major options for our destiny beyond the grave:

- We are reincarnated to live here again.
- Some immaterial essence in us – our soul – continues after we die.
- We are resurrected in some form to live beyond the grave.

To gain a sense of perspective on these options and to see what insights we can gain from the past, we turn, now, to examine early beliefs about life after death, especially those in the Old Testament which form a backdrop to the New Testament; here we discover the grounds of traditional Christian belief about the after-life.

## Notes

[1] Bryan Magee, *Confessions of a Philosopher* (New York: The Modern Library, 1999), pp. 228–29.

[2] Eberhard Bethge, *Dietrich Bonhoeffer: Theologian, Christian, Contemporary* (London: Collins, 1970), p. 830.

[3] Bertrand Russell, "Do We Survive Death?" (1936) in his *Why I am Not a Christian and Other Essays on Religion and Related Subjects* (London: Unwin, 1967), pp. 71–72.

[4] The Gifford Lectures were published as *The Varieties of Religious Experience: A Study in Human Nature* (London: Longmans, 1902), p. 524, his emphasis.

[5] Nicholas Lash, *Believing Three Ways in One God: A Reading of the Apostles' Creed* (London: SCM, 1992), p. 90.

[6] See Francis H. Cook, "*Memento Mori*: The Buddhist Thinks about Death", in *Death and Afterlife*, ed., Stephen T. Davis (Basingstoke and London: Macmillan, 1989), pp. 154–71, citing p. 163.

[7] Paul Tillich, *The Eternal Now: Sermons* (London: SCM,

1963), pp. 103, 106, 110.

[8] Kai Nielson, "The Faces of Immortality", in Stephen T. Davis, ed., *Death and Afterlife* (Basingstoke and London: Macmillan, 1989), p. 8.

[9] J. P. Moreland and Kai Nielsen, ed., *Does God Exist? The Great Debate* (Nashville: Thomas Nelson, 1990); Alvin Plantinga, *God and Other Minds: A Study of the Rational Justification of Belief in God* (Ithaca: Cornell University Press, 1990); Richard Swinburne, *The Existence of God*, 2nd ed. (Oxford: Clarendon, 1992).

[10] Cited by Colin Wilson, *Afterlife* (London: Collins/Grafton, 1987), p. 11.

[11] See, for example, Paul Kurtz, ed., *A Skeptic's Handbook of Parapsychology* (Buffalo, NY: Prometheus, 1985).

[12] Alfred Ayer, "What I Saw When I Was Dead . . .", *The Sunday Telegraph* (London, 28 August 1988), p. 5; A. J. Ayer, "Postscript to a Postmortem", *Spectator* (London, 15 October 1988), pp. 13–14.

[13] Cf. Lee W. Bailey and Jenny, ed., *The Near-death Experience: a Reader* (New York & London: Routledge, 1996).

[14] Charles Fiore and Alan Landsburg, *Death Encounters* (London: Bantam, 1979), p. 33 reported in Paul and Linda Badham, *Immortality or Extinction?* (London: Macmillan, 1982), p. 84.

[15] Ronald W. K. Paterson, *Philosophy and the Belief in a Life After Death* (London: Macmillan, 1995), p. 190.

# 2

## Where Did it All Start?

Belief in life after death, most famously among the Egyptians, is remarkably old. We will see that in all the religions we discuss, the dead continue life under the earth, often being supplied with their needs by their families still living on earth. In the light of such widespread belief we will be faced with a great puzzle in the pages of the Old Testament: almost nothing is said about life after death. Nevertheless, particularly in the Old Testament, as well as in Jewish writings around the time of Jesus, we see a fertile bed with the seeds of ideas that grew into one of the key beliefs of the Christian life.

# Where Did it All Start?

"I would rather be above ground still and working
for some poor landless man than to be lord over all
the lifeless dead"
Homer

"In my flesh I shall see God"
Job 19:26

Ideas about life after death did not begin with the resurrection of Jesus. In the Dragonbone hill caves near Beijing unmistakable indications of an idea of life after death have been found that go back to around 500,000 years ago. And, 100,000 to 25,000 years ago, Neanderthal people in Europe and surrounding areas buried their dead with food and flint instruments, probably because they thought their dead would need them in the after-life.

## The Egyptians

Of all ancient people it is the Egyptians who are best known for their interest in life after death. James H. Breasted (1865–1935), the American Egyptologist who founded the Oriental Institute at the University of Chicago, describes an incident in which he was frequently obliged to pass through the corner of a cemetery. Going up to the daily task on some neighbouring Egyptian temple in Numbia, there, directly across his path, were the feet of a dead man, buried in a shallow grave, now uncovered. To Breasted they appeared precisely like the rough and calloused feet of the workmen in the excavations. How old the grave was, he did not know. But he says that anyone familiar with the cemeteries of Egypt, ancient or modern, has found numerous bodies or portions of bodies indefinitely old, which seemed about as well preserved as those of the living. If, as Breasted assumes, this was the experience of ancient people, it must surely have stimulated a consideration of their continued existence after death.

Indeed, among ancient people who have speculated most about life after death, probably none surpass the ancient Egyptians. A cult of the dead began to develop in the so-called Naqadah (or Nakada) civilization (before c. 2925 BC). This is evident from objects found in the graveyards, such as make-up palettes, presumably useful in the after-life. In the Pyramid texts of the Old Kingdom (c. 2686–c. 2160 BC) it was the king who was the entire focus of attention for hope in a future after death, for it was he who represented the divine order of this world.

By the Middle Kingdom (c. 2040–c. 1786 BC), ideas about life after death included others besides the king. It was thought the dead continued eating, drinking, making love and working, just as they did when alive. Early in the period, all that was needed for the dead was regularly brought to the graves. From later in the period, graves are found to contain pictures and models of supplies, as if they are able to represent and provide for needs in the after-life. Eventually, all that was thought necessary was a list of things needed for those travelling beyond death.

Apart from a very early period during the Naqadah civilization, when the bones of the dead were placed in a heap in a simple grave in the sand, the idea was established that the body should be preserved intact for its role in the after-life. However, it was not believed that the body would rise again. Rather, in a way anticipating Paul 2,000 years later (see chapter 5), it was thought that, after burial, an incorruptible spiritual body, in the form of the physical one, would sprout or germinate from it.

## Mummification

In the light of the importance of the body in the after-life it is not surprising that the ancient Egyptians became well known for their mummification of the dead. However, since the mummy's lack of mobility came to be seen as a problem for life after death, there arose the expectation that Ra (or Re), the sun god and creator, would take away the bandages and call the name of the dead in order to resurrect the body.

By the time of the New Kingdom (c. 1570–c. 1085 BC), everyone was thought to have the possibility of a positive life after death in an underworld that was expected to be a duplicate of Egypt. But the dead had to pass a judgement that would be according to justice rather than wealth, although success for the just could be aided by magic.

## Mesopotamia

The literature that has survived from ancient Mesopotamia – modern Iraq – is immense, covering a period of 2,000 years and the cultures of Sumer, Babylon, Assur and Persia. We can only provide a brief glimpse of some of the beliefs about life after death as we develop a picture of thinking about the after-life in the world of the Old Testament.

The most complete Akkadian text of the so-called Gilgamesh epic is from the library of the Assyrian king Ashurbanipal, who reigned between 668 and 627 BC. Gilgamesh was a king who is supposed to have ruled at Uruk in southern Mesopotamia some time during the first half of the third millennium BC. Through the stories about him we catch glimpses of views of life after death.

The world of the dead is called the "House of Darkness" because the sun cannot reach it. It is a place of no escape where there is hunger and thirst. Well-being in the after-life depended not only on the living regularly bringing food and drink to the grave but on a proper burial. The hope of defeating death – for kings and commoners alike – was limited to the hope of an immortal name. However, Utnapishtim, the hero of this Babylonian flood story, was given a blissful and immortal life, escaping the underworld to live independent of ongoing human support at the place where the sun rises.

Also, from Ugaritic texts found at Ras Shamra on the Syrian coast opposite Cyprus, we learn of practices similar to those of the Sumerians and Akkadians. The dead were buried under homes, and water was supplied to the dead through funnels leading to the vaults. The dead were said to live in the city of the god Mot, imagined to be an insatiable abyss swallowing the dead. At night the sun goddess Shapash, ruler of the dead, travelled through the underworld with offerings for her dead subjects.

## The ancient Greeks

Death and dying were so important to the ancient Greeks that Plato (428–347 BC) reports Socrates (c. 469– c. 399 BC) saying that philosophers should study "nothing but dying and being dead" (*Phaedo* 64A). Among the Greeks there seem to have been three stages in their thinking about life after death. The earliest views were that the dead carried on a shadowy existence in their graves. They could either be a positive force for the living – if they were placated by offerings – or they could be evil forces as angry ghosts.

In the second stage (during the eighth century BC when Homer was writing) the idea of Hades developed. This was a collective dwelling-place of the dead located underground. Homer's *Iliad* begins with the spirit of Achilles sending the souls of many valiant warriors to an unconscious half-life in the inaccessible Hades, leaving them – not just their bodies – to be prey to the animals and birds. But life after death was not anticipated with any joy: "I would rather be above ground still and working for some poor landless man," says Homer, "than to be lord over all the lifeless dead" (*Odyssey* 11:487–90). Yet there are hints that heroic figures were thought to enjoy a more fulfilling after-life than others (Hesiod, *Works and Days* 166).

During the third stage of ancient Greek thinking, the dead were no longer considered always to be doomed to an under-world; they were now understood to inhabit the regions of the stars. The idea of a happier after-life for all was also enter-tained. But there was by no means a uniform view. Indeed, on the one hand, there were those such as Democritus (c. 460–370 BC) who believed that death annihilated the person. On the other hand, for some, death was not the end. For example, Antiphanes, the fourth century BC poet, had a view that is still strongly held: "We should not mourn overmuch for those who are dear to us. They are not dead; they have only gone before upon the road that all must travel. Some day we too shall come to the same way, to spend the rest of time in their society."[1]

In this period it was widely believed by the Greeks that at death the soul was released from the body. Socrates put it: "when death comes to a man, what is mortal about him, it appears, dies, but what is immortal withdraws from death and goes its way unharmed and undestroyed" (Plato, *Phaedo* 106e). Good souls flew to the upper realms. Lesser souls either hovered around the body as ghosts or were reincarnat-ed. The body, having no place in the after-life, returned to the earth, making the idea of resurrection uncomfortable if not impossible for the Greeks. For example, as Aeschylus (525/24–456/55 BC) put it, "once he is slain, there is no return to life" (*Eumenides* 647–48). Thus, as expressed much later, Greeks thought the Chaldean view fabulous that in a future world the dead would require no food and cast no shad-ow (Plutarch, *Isis and Osiris* 370C).

The views of this later Greek period are important, for they provide part of the texture of the world into which the first Christians came. We will explore these views further in a moment when we deal with thinking about life after death in the Greco-Roman world.

## The Persians

More positive hope for life after death in the world of the Old Testament came when the area was dominated by the Persians in the sixth century BC. Indeed, within literature from ancient Persia (modern Iran) we come across ideas reminiscent of those found in the later writings of the Old Testament, as well as in the New Testament.

The Persian prophet and religious reformer Zoroaster, who founded Zoroastrianism, or Parsiism as it is known in India, lived at some time between 1400 BC and 1000 BC. The *Gathas* (hymns), the only texts that can with any certainty be ascribed to Zoroaster, are permeated with references to the after-life. Upon death the soul of a person passes anxiously over the Bridge of the Separator. If the person's earthly acts and thoughts have been righteous, the bridge becomes broad so the soul can enter everlasting joy and light. This wonderful place is described as being without the discomforts of heat or cold, snow or rain, cares or tears, suffering or pain, sickness or old age, death or darkness, labour or want. However, if the person has been evil, the bridge becomes a razor's edge causing the soul to plummet into the regions of horror and darkness where there is wailing and poor food.

Yet, in Persian thought, which may be echoed in the Old Testament (Daniel 12:1–3), more dominant than what happens immediately after death was the belief that at the end of time there would be a general resurrection of the dead. This was to be followed by a final judgement which would separate evil people from the good people who go on to enjoy a never-ending renewed world.[2]

## The Greco-Romans

Views abroad during the so-called Greco-Roman period are particularly interesting to us, for they are the ideas of people shared or known by those who were writing the books and letters that are now part of the New Testament.

Two options taken up in the Greco-Roman world had been spelt out long previously by Plato: "A dead person is either the same as nothing, not having any kind of sensation of anything, or, death is the removal and relocation of the soul from here to another place" (*Apology* 40C).

1. "*I was not, I was; I am not, I don't care!*" Epicurus (341–270 BC) remained influential in the world of Paul. The same can be said of Zeno (335–263 BC), the founder of the more popular Stoicism (compare Acts 17:18). Both schools of thought taught that there was nothing after death. Epicurus put it: "Death is nothing to us; for what has been dissolved has no sensation, and what has no sensation is nothing to us" (*Principal Doctrine* 2). Epitaphs reflecting this view have been found from around the time of the writing of the New Testament. One often repeated is the saying: "I was not, I was; I am not, I don't care!"[3] This denial of an after-life led to the view that life was to be enjoyed to the full while it lasted, a view still in force when Luke was writing about Paul's time in Athens (Acts 17:18–20) and around in the Sanhedrin in Jerusalem (Acts 23:8). When we examine Judaism (see below) we will see that this view was also shared by the Sadducees.

2. *But the soul lives on.* While Plato the student may have been ambivalent, as we have seen earlier in this chapter, Socrates the teacher was decisive: he thought that when death came what was mortal in us died. What was immortal and imperishable withdrew from death and went its way

unharmed and undestroyed (Plato, *Phaedo* 106e). From this, the view developed that good souls flew to the upper regions to live in celestial bliss apart from the body; for some this was a joining in the life of the gods (Sirach 45). Lesser souls were thought to hover around the earth as ghosts to be purified before, perhaps, returning to another bodily existence. But the idea that the after-life involved the body being resurrected was not seriously considered: bodies were burned so as to release the ascending soul (Lucian, *Peregrinus* 6, 30, 33).

For most Greco-Romans resurrection was impossible; the dead are not raised (Plutarch, *Romulus* 28:4, 6–8), not even with a body that casts no shadow nor needs food or drink, as the Chaldeans anticipated (Plutarch, *Isis and Osiris* 370C). However, it was not only into this thought world that the early Christian writers were making their way. Importantly, Christians were also developing their thinking in the light of the Judaism of the period, which we will come to in a moment.

## So far . . .

As we have seen, not all ancients believed in an after-life. Juvenal (c. 55–c. 140 AD), the Roman lawyer and satirist, attacked the idea: "Not even a child believes that there are ghosts and realms below the earth and a punt pole plying among black fogs in the Stygian river and so many thousands crossing in a single boat" (*Satires* 2:149–52). Similarly, Lucretius (c. 99–55 BC), the Roman poet and philosopher, would have nothing to do with the idea of the immortality of the soul: "As mist and smoke disperse into the air, you can be certain that the soul also is dispersed and perishes much more quickly, breaking up into its original atoms" (*De Rerum Natura* 3:436–38).

Yet, common to all the religions we have surveyed is the view that while death is powerful and final, the dead go to a world that is (generally) underneath the earth and reflects that of the living. In some cases this reflection includes the continuation of the social hierarchy found among the living. Another simple and common view of the after-life was that life – however shadowy – would continue with the ongoing support of the living. Some cultures saw death as allowing the spirit to escape to the after-life; others took a more holistic view, including the whole person in the after-life. From our discussions we could say that the idea of a distinction in the after-life between good and bad people (to put it crudely), along with some form of judgement, came relatively late, as did the idea of a general resurrection of the dead.

For most ancients, while the spirit and body can be separated, the spirit cannot find rest unless the body is buried and sustained correctly by the living. Later beliefs reduced the importance of the body so that death became the liberation of the soul to take up its reward or punishment. Some considered it was possible to escape the world of the dead for a time, especially to take part in feasts in their honour. Also, the dead could enter the world of the living as stars or birds, or, as ghosts, could continue to influence the living. Some individuals were thought to be able to avoid death by being taken away by the gods to live for ever somewhere between earth and the world of the dead. We have just noted the distinctive Persian belief that at the end of time there would be a general resurrection of the dead, now familiar to us in the New Testament.

We have seen that there was widespread belief about the after-life in all the cultures we surveyed. We have even seen hints of beliefs that we will meet in the New Testament. In the light of this fertility of thought we are confronted by a great surprise and puzzle in the pages of the Old Testament.

## The Old Testament

The great surprise for us in the Old Testament is this: there is markedly much less discussion about the after-life than in the literature of surrounding religions – to the point that the Old Testament writers are remarkably restrained, even reluctant or negligent, in exploring themes relating to life after death.

It is only through a close reading of the Old Testament that we can detect evidence of beliefs about the after-life, including about such widely held ideas among surrounding people that the spirits of the dead are able to help the living (Deuteronomy 18:11; Isaiah 19:3), and that the dead may escape back into the world of the living as birds (compare Isaiah 8:19).

*Death*

Rather surprisingly, as ancient Israel's religion developed, death came to be seen not as the beginning of another life but as total extinction. One of Job's friends says that people "will perish for ever like their own dung" (Job 20:7). Job himself expected his death to lead to gloom and deep darkness (10:21). In Genesis 3:19 God says that we are dust and will return to dust (compare Job 10:9). According to this view, there is no soul separate from the body that will survive death: human beings are animated bodies, not incarnate souls.

Even as late as Ecclesiasticus (or Ben Sirach, written c. 180 BC) the view persisted among some Jews that there was no life after death: "Give, and take, and indulge yourself, because in Hades one cannot look for luxury. All living beings become old like a garment, for the decree from of old is, 'You must die!'" (Sirach 14:16–17). The only way a person could live beyond death was through having children (30:4–5) or a good reputation (41:11–13). Ecclesiastes 12:7 says that "the dust returns to the earth as it was, and the breath (or spirit) returns to God who gave it."[4] But even this is not a belief that the soul or spirit will survive death, only that God is taking back his life-giving spirit. Thus what, if anything, survives death is not a part of a person but a shadowy reflection of the whole person.

## Sheol

Although it is notoriously difficult to date Old Testament writings, some of the earliest views on the after-life seem to revolve around the concept of Sheol, which is mentioned 66 times. In contrast to the detailed descriptions of the world of the dead in other ancient texts, we have few details of Sheol, though what we have is quite wide-ranging.

The earliest mentions of Sheol imply that it was a place for the dead below the earth (for example, Genesis 37:35; Numbers 16:30). It was the lowest place imaginable (Deuteronomy 32:22; Isaiah 7:11), back through whose gates and snares (2 Samuel 22:6) it was impossible to escape (Job 7:9; Psalm 89:48). Sheol was often associated with images of water (Jonah 2:3–6). Sometimes Sheol is pictured as a place of ignorance where the dead know nothing of what is happening on earth (Job 14:21; Ecclesiastes 9:5, 10). In other references the dead appear to be aware of the living (Isaiah 14:10–11). As if swallowed up by its insatiable appetite,[5] both the good (Genesis 37:35) and the bad (Numbers 16:30) go to what is sometimes pictured as a corporate life (Isaiah 14:10). Sometimes those in Sheol are portrayed as completely isolated from God; other passages are more positive about an ongoing contact with God.[6]

Sheol is particularly associated with premature or evil deaths, leaving others on their death to be reunited with their relatives in an unspecified place. Sometimes Sheol seems to level social rank (compare Job 21:2–26); other times it appears to reflect such earthly distinctions (compare 1 Samuel 28:14; Isaiah 14:9). What details we have of Sheol do not form a tidy or consistent picture. But it is clearly not a place of worthwhile existence beyond death (Ecclesiastes 9:10).

## The puzzle

From this brief survey of life after death in the Old Testament we are bound to ask why the Old Testament writers seem to have been surprisingly reluctant to develop ideas of life after death. This puzzling lack of interest in a belief in an after-life – even to the point of its denial – may have come about in a number of ways. First, it could be that the concept of an after-life, at least as visualized in Sheol, was not a worthwhile existence for the dead.[7] Or, secondly, perhaps Old Testament writers were reacting against the Egyptian hope that life after death was to be associated with the dying and rising of Osiris, the Egyptian god of the dead and ruler of the underworld. We can be fairly confident that Egyptian ideas were both known[8] and modified[9] by Old Testament traditions. Or, thirdly, it could be that the living were not to meddle with the dead, who had entered another world over which God had control (compare Deuteronomy 26:14).

Alternatively, there is a fourth and important factor that could have led to the decreasing belief in life after death. It may be detected in the story of Saul consulting the witch of Endor (1 Samuel 28:1–25). The dead Samuel who appears coming up out of the ground is called a divine being or god, and he knows Saul's future. Given its many prohibitions, necromancy (the use of mediums to call up the dead) was probably a practice widespread amongst the Israelites.[10] In that this practice of necromancy is outlawed, not only calling up the dead to listen to them instead of God for direction, but the very continued life of the dead may have been thought to be a threat to the Israelites' closely guarded monotheism.

Since the Israelites were discouraged from turning to necromancy and speculating about the after-life, we probably have the reason why the Old Testament writers explore the meaning of life on this earth with a degree of sophistication unparalleled amongst neighbouring people. For example, the so-called Wisdom literature in the Bible (Job, Proverbs and Ecclesiastes) celebrates the potential of a full life on earth, as it does in its healthy materialism, the dignity of the body, and the common sense of morality contributing to a full, happy and controlled life. The healthy eroticism of the Song of Songs and the blessing of a long life (compare Psalm 21:4) may also be a by-product of the value placed on the present life. But this lack of interest in life after death was not where the thinking of God's people remained.

## A way forward

Seeds of belief in life after death can be seen later in the Old Testament literature. One of these was probably the ongoing belief that God had power over death (Deuteronomy 32:39; 1 Samuel 2:6). This included the belief that God could rescue the terminally ill (Psalms 30:3; 116:8), as well as "take up" people to heaven without them having to die, as in the cases of Enoch and Elijah (Genesis 5:24; 2 Kings 2:1–18).

Another of the seeds of belief in life after death probably came with the increased understanding of God's relationship with us as individuals. It may have been true on a national level that there was a direct relationship between virtue and blessing, or evil and destruction. But from an individual's perspective this direct relationship is not seen early in Old Testament religion (compare Ecclesiastes 2:12–17). God was understood to have entered into a relationship – a covenant – with the nation as a whole, not with individuals.

Then, however, most clearly and famously expressed in Jeremiah, it was understood that God related to individuals (Jeremiah 31:31–34). Implications of this conviction can be seen in Job. At one point Job asks if mortals will live again

(Job 14:14). He answers his own question by saying that God does not call to the dead but destroys their hope (14:19). Yet, further on, Job expresses his hope that he will see God after he dies (19:25–27). Based on his trust in God, he cannot conceive that his God will not vindicate him – as an individual. Indeed, three times here, Job repeats that he expects to see God; "seeing him" being a description of an intimate relationship with God (compare Psalms 11:7; 27:4). What had been said in Psalm 17:15 of seeing God in this life (or of having an intimate relationship with him) is now said by Job to be his expectation beyond death. More details of the after-life Job does not give us, for Job is not declaring a developed theology but expressing a spontaneous cry for help, arising out of his hope in God.

This embryonic hope in an after-life developed along two lines. However, we must keep in mind that there is much variety in Old Testament thought, not the tidy lines of consistency or development for which we might wish.

## 1. Immortality

Even though immortality – survival beyond death – was not a strong belief for long periods of the history of God's people, hints of the idea of immortality can be detected in early material in the Old Testament.

### Samuel

For example, we have seen a belief in the continued existence of the dead in the prohibitions of necromancy (Deuteronomy 18:10–13), and in the story of Saul calling up Samuel (1 Samuel 28:1–25). Also, after Saul had been wounded and defeated by the Philistines and, along with his three sons and those with him, had committed suicide, the Philistines decapitated Saul and hung his naked body on the wall of Bethshan. Probably expressing belief in an after-life, courageous men from Jabeshgilead took down the bodies and buried them (1 Samuel 31:1–13). Further, the prophet Amos condemns the people of Moab for cremating the king of Edom (Amos 2:1). Implicit in these two stories is the idea that a person could still be injured after death; the person was still experiencing some form of consciousness. Also, it is implied that, after death, people were believed to have their bodies. The body was probably thought to be a replica of the earthly body, a view spelt out clearly very much later in the first century AD (compare *Apocalypse of Moses* 40:1–7).

Though important for our theme, the psalms are often ambiguous when they express hope in an after-life. Sometimes it could be that they are expressing a hope to avoid death, as did Enoch and Elijah (Genesis 5:24; 2 Kings 2:1–18). In other psalms, especially those known as songs of individual lament or of thanksgiving, the hope is probably that God will rescue people from death and Sheol through rescuing them from distresses and threats in this life and allow them to go on living so that praise of him can continue.[11] But this is not always the case. There are four psalms which still remain the focus of attention for biblical scholars – and which warrant our attention – in trying to understand what the Old Testament says about life after death.

### Psalm 16

At first sight the writer of Psalm 16:10 seems to be expressing the hope that he will meet God after death: "For you do not give me up to Sheol, or let your faithful one see the Pit." However, it could be that the writer is crying out for protection from harm (16:1–2) and expressing his hope that God will preserve him from untimely death and show him "the path of life" (16:11; compare Proverbs 2:19).

### Psalms 49 and 73

These two psalms are also not without ambiguity, but they do deal more directly with life beyond death. Psalm 49:15 says, "God will ransom my soul from the power of Sheol, for he will receive me" (49:15). This cannot be expressing the hope of avoiding death as did Enoch and Elijah (Genesis 5:24; 2 Kings 2:1), for the writer is not expecting to avoid death (Psalm 49:10). Rather, he is probably expecting that death will not sever his relationship with God. This psalm is also clear about the fate of the foolhardy: instead of God, "death shall be their shepherd" (49:14; contrast 23:1, 4). Also, the rich cannot expect their present life to continue: they shall "never again see the light" (49:19). In some places the psalms more clearly express an expectation that after death they will see God rather than be left in Sheol.

Where Psalm 73:24 says, "You guide me with your counsel, and afterward you will receive me with honour", the writer could have in mind being vindicated in this life. However, ambiguity here is attenuated by the writer's faith that God is his "for ever" (73:26) which, most probably, includes more than this life.

## Psalm 103

This psalm provides an example of a reference to life after death in a comment about being rescued in this life. God is said to heal and (therefore) ransom a person from the pit of death (Psalm 103:3–5). This is clearly a reference to being preserved from death. But the following reference to God renewing the person's youth "like the eagle's" (103:5) – probably an echo of the phoenix, an Egyptian symbol of rejuvenation – is most likely a hint of life beyond death.[12]

There are certainly inklings of immortality in the Old Testament, notably in these psalms.[13] But with the ambiguity they contain, it is obvious that no clear doctrine of the afterlife had been established. What we have in the Old Testament are only glimpses of various tentative beliefs in immortality. These have arisen from the confidence of Old Testament writers that the relationship already established by God with the individual is so significant that it will not be broken by death but continued beyond it.

In view of our later discussions about life after death it is worth noting two important points.

- None of the Old Testament writers suggest that there is anything about human beings that is destined naturally to continue after death. According to the Old Testament, in and of itself human life is destined to end at death. Life beyond the grave depends entirely on God – as a gift – continuing the relationship he has established with people.
- Life after death is generally seen to involve the whole person rather than an essence or soul or spirit naturally surviving death without the body.

However, as we are about to see, immortality or immediate survival in another world beyond death was not the only expression of the hope that God's relationship with his people would survive the grave.

## 2. Resurrection of the dead

The Old Testament has a great deal to say about resurrection involving Israel as a whole. We find the metaphors of death and resurrection of the nation as a whole in the famous vision of dry bones coming back together and living, in Ezekiel 37. Also, in Hosea 6:2 the prophet encourages the people to return to the Lord for "on the third day he will raise us up" (see also Hosea 13:14). There is, further, the hope expressed by the prophet Isaiah that God "will swallow up death for ever" (Isaiah 25:7). But the Old Testament has very little to say about the dead individual being resurrected – individuals returning to the present life to live again among the living. Unfortunately, the few passages we can find on the subject are not all as clear in meaning as at first might be thought.

Some scholars hold the view that there was an anticipation of individual resurrection early in the history of the Israelites, perhaps borrowed from the Egyptians before the exodus. The majority view, however, is that the idea of an individual being resurrected came late into the literature of the Old Testament. We shall discuss the pertinent passages in the order they are generally agreed to have been written, beginning with Deuteronomy and Samuel, part of the so-called Deuteronomic material which came to its present form in the sixth century BC. From these passages we are trying to glean what, if anything, the writers may have understood about life after death.

## Deuteronomy 32:39

This verse contains the line: "there is no god beside me. I kill and I make alive." By itself, this could suggest that God is able to bring a person back to life. However, the verse immediately continues with a parallel: "I wound and I heal." This parallelling of phrases, common in Hebrew, shows that what is probably in mind is what we found in some of the Psalms: not that God is expected to raise a person to return to this life but that he will deliver a person from mortal peril.

## 1 Samuel 2:6

Here the Song of Hannah (1 Samuel 2:1–11) includes the words: "The Lord kills and brings to life; he brings down to Sheol and raises up." Once again, on a first reading, this could be taken to mean that God restores the dead to life. However, the next and parallel verse says, "The Lord makes poor and makes rich", which quite likely means that God makes one person poor and another rich, rather than makes a person poor and then rich. Thus the idea of God killing and bringing to life is quite likely to mean that God causes death and causes birth.

### Job 19:26

From perhaps 600 years before Christ comes the book of Job, an ancient Hebrew poem. Its most celebrated passage, which also may help us, was immortalized by an air in Handel's *Messiah*. Unfortunately, the verse is obscure and difficult to interpret. The line that is of interest to us says: "and after my skin has been thus destroyed, then in my flesh shall I see God." This could refer to Job's present life, or it could refer to his being resurrected to see God. We can only conclude that perhaps the ambiguity was deliberate at a time when ideas of an after-life through resurrection were at their most embryonic and uncertain (see 14:1–22).

### Isaiah 26:19

With the prophets of a later time we begin to see more clearly the hope expressed not only that one day there will be a life after death, but that there will be a resurrection. The most renowned statement comes in the so-called "Apocalypse of Isaiah" (Isaiah 24–27), perhaps composed in the third century BC. The statement affirms that one day, "Your dead shall live, their [or my] corpses shall rise" (Isaiah 26:19; compare 25:7). Since this saying comes in a passage with a collective interest, what at first seems a statement that individuals will rise to life could well be a hope that the community as a whole will be reborn (compare Ezekiel 37:1–14). However, in the second phrase, "their [or my] corpses shall arise", there is embedded the seeds of hope for the resurrection of the individual, not only of the nation as a whole, as in Ezekiel 37. But, it is not a universal resurrection that is in mind.

As we will see in a moment, the view that everyone would be raised from the dead came hesitantly and much later – in Judaism. Instead, the verse we are looking at implies that only those who belong to God will be restored to life. We can also note that there is no concept here of the possibility of disembodied life. The restoration to life is not just of a soul. Return to life presupposes no less than the revivification of the body from the sleep of death.

We can draw attention to the same point that arose when we were dealing with the beginnings of belief in immortality. That is, life after death through the resurrection of our bodies is not based on any inherent qualities in those who have died nor in some aspect of the human being which can be expected to surpass death. Rather, the dead live because of God's action: God sends his "radiant dew" (Isaiah 26:19b), dew here playing the role of God's Spirit in Ezekiel (Ezekiel 37:14).

## Daniel 12:1-3

For our topic, this is the most important passage in the Old Testament. It is not until this passage from the middle of the second century BC that we come to the one explicit, unambiguous reference to an after-life in the whole of the Old Testament. Probably written during the Maccabean revolt (167–143 BC), the book of Daniel encourages faith and resistance through stories of loyalty which bring deliverance, even after death.[14] Perhaps with Isaiah 26:19 in mind, Daniel expresses the clear hope of a resurrected life after death:

> But at that time your people shall be delivered, everyone who is found written in the book. Many of those who sleep in the dust of the earth shall awake, some to everlasting life, and some to shame and everlasting contempt. Those who are wise shall shine like the brightness of the sky, and those who lead many to righteousness, like the stars forever and ever (Daniel 12:1–3).

The scene here is of the unprecedented distress expected during the final chapter of human history. Once again we have a writer not anticipating a universal resurrection (compare Isaiah 26:19). Instead, God's people or "everyone who is found written in the book" – both the wicked and the righteous – shall be delivered (Daniel 12:1). Surprisingly, at first sight, our author does not go on to say that "all" of God's people shall be raised. Rather, "many" (12:2) shall awake, some to everlasting life and some to everlasting contempt. This could mean that the best and worst of God's people are in mind, the indifferent remaining in the dust of the earth. More likely, in filling out the previous verse, the "many" among all those who have died refers only to God's people who will be resurrected to everlasting life. In the following verse this is spelt out: the wise are expected to be like stars (12:3). As stars and angels had long been taken to be the same (compare Isaiah 14:12), it can be assumed that the reward being handed out to the wise was for them to be angels, members of the heavenly court. Nothing is said of the reward for the others, save that they will be rewarded with shame and everlasting contempt.

What is in view here in Daniel 12:1–3 are not individual experiences of life after death, nor a universal resurrection. Rather Daniel imagines a general resurrection at least of God's people – both the wicked and the righteous. What is envisaged for people is a return to physical life to stand side by side in this world with those who have not yet died. Going beyond the hints and expectations of earlier times, the writer expects not only the wise but also others to be raised, in order to receive their less favourable rewards.

This view of life after death is so different from anything we have so far encountered that it is likely to have arisen not only from outside influence (perhaps reflected in Persian thinking – see above) but also from the author's reflection on his faith in God to vindicate the faithful and punish the unfaithful. When we come to examine ideas of resurrection in chapter 5 we will see that this passage – or at least the views it carries – had some influence on the New Testament as well as later views on life after death.

## Judaism[15]

From our brief examination of the relevant Old Testament texts we can see that up until around the second century BC probably only a small number of God's people would have believed in life after death. Those who did contemplate living beyond their grave shared the prevailing view of ancient people that life after death would be a shadowy, ghostly existence in the underworld, which Old Testament writers called Sheol. However – and remarkably – within a couple of centuries of the last writings of the Old Testament, most Jews appear to have had clear and strong views about life after death.

Further, as the writings we have that deal with life after death do not seem to be arguing in the face of disbelief, the views we come across can be taken to have been widespread. Why the late Old Testament views developed so rapidly and became so widespread at this time is unclear: it could have been a response to the fact that the Maccabean martyrs were dying without seeing any vindication for their beliefs while their persecutors were triumphing.[16] In any case, despite the great diversity of views, some common threads can be detected in the Judaism of the period, which formed the cradle of Christianity.

### Body and soul

We have seen that what hints there are of belief in life after death in the Old Testament involved the whole person. This was in contrast to the Greeks who thought that at death the soul was released to live for ever. In Judaism, by the time of the writing of the New Testament, this was changing so that at death body and soul were thought to be separated. What happened then was the cause of great speculation. At least for some Jews, the soul went to Sheol, known as "the chambers of the souls". The body stayed in the tomb to await the resurrection when body and soul would be reunited. In this there are echoes of Greek dualism but with a marked and important difference: souls in Sheol only experience life when body and soul are reunited at the resurrection.

## Resurrection: Israel and individuals

Although, later in the period, individualism came to dominate thinking about the after-life in Judaism, anticipating life after death was generally a hope of rising to life to join in the fulfilment of God's promises for the nation of Israel as a whole. Thus, at death it was thought individuals did not experience their final destiny. Instead they expected to wait in various places in Sheol – some places for the wicked and some for the righteous – until the general resurrection and final judgement at the end of time (2 Maccabees 7:9, 14; 12:44). Nevertheless, apparently in the light of a preliminary tribunal, people already knew what their destiny would be at the final judgement. There was, therefore, already delight in suffering, in anticipation (*1 Enoch* 22; 4 Ezra 7:75–101) of the personal and general resurrection. In this resurrection the wicked would be transformed into a worse condition, and the righteous into glorious splendour (*2 Baruch* 49:1–51:1). As time went by, the tendency was to heighten the expectation of this preliminary bliss to the point where the most common view was that at death souls went straight to paradise. For some Jews, this was true for only the great men of God: Enoch, Moses and Elijah (4 Ezra 14:9), for example. For other Jews, only the "just" (those in a right relationship with God) would be raised to life; the rest would remain in their graves.[17]

## Judgement

For some, the last judgement was expected after the messianic age – the age when God's special messenger would reign; for others it came before.[18] In any case, it was generally thought that sentence would be passed on the whole of mankind (*2 Baruch* 51:4–5; 4 Ezra 7:37). The wicked were expected to be cast into the fire of Gehenna[19], which was generally seen to be for ever,[20] though some understood it to be only for a limited time.[21] The lack of certainty or clarity on these issues is captured in the Dead Sea Scrolls where the wicked are said to be destroyed as well as suffering eternally (*The Community Rule* [1QS] 4:11–14). It is important that we note this, for we will see the same ambivalence – perhaps paradox – in the New Testament (see chapter 7), and even in some thinking today.

## Raised to glory

We have already had cause to quote the famous sentence in Daniel 12:3: "Those who are wise shall shine like the brightness of the sky . . . like the stars for ever and ever." Perhaps on the basis of this idea, many writers took up the view that the righteous dead would rise to shine like stars because they were rising to share the undying life of the heavenly beings, who were understood to be bright and shining (*1 Enoch* 104:2; *2 Baruch* 51:10). Since one group of the members of the bright heavenly bodies were the angels, it is not surprising that the righteous dead were thought to be (or be like) the angels (*2 Baruch* 51:5, 10, 12). However, these resurrected people were sometimes said to live on a transformed earth rather than in the heavens.[22] To this important idea we shall return in chapter 8.

What, however, was thought to happen to the large majority of people who were neither totally righteous nor totally evil? Those who followed the teacher Shammai (first century AD) maintained that going down to hell healed or purged them (compare Zechariah 13:9); those of the more liberal school of Hillel of the same period held that God, in his great mercy (compare Exodus 34:6; Psalm 116), would incline the balance to the side of mercy, not sending them to Gehenna at all.[23]

## Reincarnation

There is also a rather surprising view to be found in the

Judaism of the time of the New Testament: reincarnation. Flavius Josephus (37–c. 100 AD) was a Jewish soldier, politician and historian writing at the same time as the gospel writers. He says that the Pharisees maintained that every soul is imperishable, but only the souls of spotless and law-abiding persons are allotted the most holy place in heaven. From there – in the revolution that was expected to mark the transition between this age and the age to come – these souls are expected to make an easy return to earth to find chaste bodies to inhabit. This left the souls of the wicked to suffer eternal punishment or imprisonment.[24] But, so far as we can tell from the literature of the time, few Jews believed in reincarnation.

## Two exceptions

When we turn to the New Testament, the notable thing about the dominant views on the after-life in Judaism is that they were largely shared by the early Christians. Like other Jews of the time, the earliest Christians saw their ideas as arising out of their Scriptures.

One group that held different views about life after death in Judaism were the Sadducees: a small body of politically and economically influential aristocratic families. Josephus says they thought that the soul perishes along with the body: "As for the persistence of the soul after death, penalties in the underworld, and rewards, they will have none of them."[25] Since the Pentateuch (the first five books of the Old Testament) was their only Scripture, the Sadducees' rejection of an after-life is not surprising. The Pentateuch does not deal with the issue. How far the Sadducees reflected the views of ordinary people we cannot be certain, though in the light of the wealth of literature reflecting beliefs related to life after death, their views were probably relatively confined and uncommon.

Another group of people whose views on life after death seem to have been at a tangent to the generally accepted

views of the time were the Essenes of the Qumran community. Even though they were familiar with the book of Daniel
(fragments of the book have been found at Qumran), there is
no hint of the idea of resurrection among the writing of the
Qumran people. Instead, as Josephus tells us, the Essenes took
up the Greek view of the soul surviving death. Along with
some other Jews (compare Wisdom 3:1–5:16), the Essenes
believed the immortal soul was entangled in the prison-house
of the body. At death the soul was liberated to be borne aloft.
The scrolls themselves tell us that members of the Qumran
community were raised to an everlasting height and joined the
everlasting community of the Sons of Heaven (*Thanksgiving
Hymns* [1QH] 3:20–22). According to Josephus, the Essenes
believed that virtuous souls went to a pleasant place beyond
the sea. Other souls were relegated "to a murky and tempestu-
ous dungeon, big with never-ending punishment" (*Jewish War*
2:155).

## Conclusions

From what we have seen in this chapter, we cannot for one
moment think that the origins of ideas about life after death
were monopolized by those represented in the Old Testament,
nor even by the New Testament. Indeed, we have noted
unmistakable indications of belief in life after death from very
early times, as well as across all the major cultures that
formed the cradle of life reflected in the Old Testament and
then in early Christianity. Even the idea that life after death
would involve resurrection was not the exclusive province of
the biblical writers but, most probably, something they borrowed from their neighbours.

Rather surprisingly, Old Testament writers seem to have
been reluctant to take up and develop ideas of life after death.
When, all around them, others were speculating about life
after death, for most of their history God's people appeared to

show almost no interest in life after death. Indeed, for some time in the history of Israelite religion, death came to be seen as the end. We saw that this could have been because it was thought that allowing the dead to live on would compromise their monotheism. It could also be that they did not think there was a worthwhile view of life after death available that would do justice to the integrity of the relationship God had initiated with his people in this life. When we do find ideas of life after death among the earliest Old Testament writings, generally in descriptions of the underworld of Sheol, they bear little resemblance to the detailed and developed beliefs of the various Mesopotamian peoples we surveyed.

Save for Daniel 12:1–3, the hints of immortality and particularly resurrection which we saw emerge later in the writings of the Old Testament remain enigmatic at best. So, not only were Old Testament writers late and reluctant in taking up views on the after-life, but what views we can recover are remarkably underdeveloped compared with, for example, those we have noted from Egypt or the Persians.

In all of this we can see that – in contrast to how we may see ourselves as naturally immortal (see chapters 1 and 4) – from the perspective of Old Testament writers, there is nothing about us that means we can expect an after-life. It is not even believed that we have souls that can live on unaffected by our death. For, at death, God withdraws his Spirit, leaving the person to die and return to the earth as dust. We have seen that, for Old Testament writers, the expectation that we can live beyond death arises in considering the mercy and justice of God. That is, if the loving relationship God has established with his people during this life is of any significance to him it could not be terminated by death. In other words, if God as our loving Father seeks to draw us into a perfect relationship with him we can expect that relationship to extend beyond this short and incomplete earthly life.

## The next step?

In the first chapter I tried to make a case that it is more than reasonable for us to anticipate life after death. In this chapter we have seen that such beliefs are very ancient and various. While the Old Testament is strangely all but silent about life after death, by the time the New Testament was being written there was a blossoming of belief about life beyond the grave among God's people. Indeed, we have seen that the range of views expressed at the time of the writing of the New Testament is similar to what we find today. Some people thought that death was the end; some expected to be reincarnated; for some an after-life was dependent on having an immortal soul; others placed their hopes in resurrection.

We turn now to examine these principal ideas, for they are still of great interest in our time. We will be seeking to test these beliefs in the light of our experience, as well as for their internal strength and consistency. Also, we will be scrutinizing these views from a biblical perspective. We begin with the popular belief in reincarnation.

## Notes

[1] Cited by Peter G. Bolt, "Life, Death, and the Afterlife in the Greco-Roman World", in Richard N. Longenecker, ed., *Life in the Face of Death: The Resurrection Message of the New Testament* (Grand Rapids, MI and Cambridge, UK: Eerdmans, 1998), p. 69.

[2] See Mary Boyce, *Zoroastrians* (London: Routledge, 1979); Bernhard Lang, "Afterlife: Ancient Israel's Changing Vision of the World Beyond", *Bible Review* 4 (1988), p. 19.

[3] Cited by Bolt, in Longenecker, ed., *Life in the Face of Death*, p. 68. See also Cicero, *Letters to Atticus* 12:18:1; Horace, *Odes* 4:7:15–17; Seneca, *Letters* 54:4.

[4] Compare Genesis 2:7; 6:3; 35:18; Job 33:4, 14; Psalm 104:29.

[5] Isaiah 5:14; Habakkuk 2:5; Proverbs 27:20; 30:15b–16.

[6] See Psalms 30:9–10; 88:5–6; 115:17 and also Psalm 139:8; Amos 9:2.

[7] Jonah 2:3–6; Job 17:11–16; Psalms 31:17–18; 115:17.

[8] For example, 1 Kings 6:18, 29, 32, 34-35.

[9] Job 16:19–22; 19:25–27; 31.

[10] Leviticus 19:26; 20:6, 27; Deuteronomy 18:10–11; 1 Samuel 28:3, 9; Isaiah 8:19; 19:3.

[11] Compare Psalms 9:13–15; 30:4–10; 40:3–4; 56:13; 71:20–24; 107:20–22; 116:8–10, 17–19.

[12] Other Old Testament passages which deal with the present life but may have implications for life after death are Isaiah 26:7–19; 52:13–53:12; Ezekiel 37:1–14.

[13] Compare Psalms 17:15; 23:6; 139:18.

[14] Compare 2 Maccabees 7:9, 14, 23, 36. On the complex origin of Daniel, as we have it, see J. E. Goldingay, *Daniel* (Dallas, TX.: Word, 1989), pp. 320–29.

[15] "Judaism" is the term generally used for Jewish culture extending from the end of the Old Testament through to after the writing of the New Testament. Further on our topic, see Richard Bauckham, "Life, Death, and the Afterlife in Second Temple Judaism", in Longenecker, ed., *Life in the Face of Death*, pp. 80–95.

[16] Compare 2 Maccabees 7:9–29; 12:43–45; 14:36.

[17] *Psalms of Solomon* 3:16; 14:2–4; Josephus, *Antiquities of the Jews* 18:14; *Jewish War* 2:163.

[18] Compare *2 Baruch* 50:4; 4 Ezra 7:33–44; 6:1–17 and Daniel 12:2.

[19] *2 Baruch* 44:15; 51:1–2, 4; 6; 4 Ezra 7:36–38, 84.

[20] Isaiah 66:24; Daniel 12:2; *Testament of Zebulon* 10; *Testament of Reuben* 5:5; *The Community Rule* [1QS] 4:12–13; Josephus, *Jewish War* 2:163; *Antiquities of the Jews* 18:14.

[21] Compare Mishnah, *Eduyyot* 2:10; Babylonian Talmud, *Nedarim* 8b.

[22] Compare *1 Enoch* 104:2; *2 Baruch* 51:10; *Testament of Moses* 10:9–10 and *1 Enoch* 45:4–5; 51:5; *Sibylline Oracles* 4:187.

[23] Tosephta, *Sanhedrin* 13:3; *Rosh ha-Shanah* 16b–17a.

[24] Josephus, *Jewish War* 3:374; compare 2:163; *Against Apion* 2:218; *Jewish Antiquities* 18:12–14.

[25] Josephus, *Jewish War* 2:166; compare *Jewish Antiquities* 18:16; Acts 23:8.

# 3

## Do We Come Back to This Life?

It is now fashionable to believe that after we die we will come back to this life in some form. But what is the evidence for reincarnation, or transmigration of souls, as it is also called? To assess the truth of reincarnation we will have to look especially at a moral argument along with the argument from what twins experience, as well as the supposed empirical evidence. Some people have argued that the Bible teaches that we come back to this life. Others have suggested that the Bible has been censored of references that originally taught reincarnation. We will discover that while there may be nothing intrinsically impossible about reincarnation, there are such large logical and moral problems with the idea, that any clear-thinking person will not consider reincarnation as a reasonable expectation of what happens to us after we die.

# Do We Come Back to This Life?

"Just as a person casts off worn-out garments and
puts on others that are new, even so does the
embodied soul cast off worn-out bodies
and take on others that are new"
The *Bhagavad Gita* 2:22

Reincarnation is "fitting for the chatter of frogs
and jackdaws, the stupidity of fishes,
or the insensibility of trees"
Gregory of Nyssa

Some people stake their lives on reincarnation. On 7 December 1977, Eldon McCorkhill, 33, and Linda Cummings, 28, were sitting in a bar in Redlands, California. They were drinking and chatting. The conversation turned to the subject of life after death. Linda told Eldon that she was firmly convinced of the reality of reincarnation. Eldon scoffed loudly, and a spirited debate ensued. The argument continued as they travelled back to McCorkhill's apartment. Once there, he pulled a loaded pistol out of a drawer and handed it to her. "If you believe in this, let's see what you'll come back as," he said. Linda took the gun, pointed it at her head and pulled the trigger.[1]

The belief that we are involved in a cyclical series of rebirths, continually returning to this life – perhaps as, or in, an insect, animal or human body – in order to suffer and so be purged of evil, is widely seen as a realistic option for life after death. According to the 1982 Gallup poll, 23% of the United States population believe in some form of reincarnation. It has been suggested that the figure is 18% of the population for

Britain. And perhaps one third to one half of the world's population hold some form of reincarnation as part of their belief system. Sylvester Stallone believes he was once a monkey in Central America. Shirley MacLaine passionately advocates reincarnation through films and books. Also, Eastern religions, some with their strong belief in reincarnation, are playing an increasingly important role in Western thinking and religion. Further, we saw hints in the last chapter that reincarnation has a centuries-long history. Therefore, as reincarnation is no longer an approach to life after death reserved for the lunatic fringe, it is important in our thinking clearly about life after death that we understand this philosophy and evaluate it from a Christian perspective.

Is reincarnation only "fitting for the chatter of frogs and fishes", as Gregory of Nyssa (c. 330–c. 395 AD) said, or "a most comforting explanation of reality", as Albert Schweitzer (1875–1965) claimed? In a book of this size and scope we will have to confine our discussion to a modest interaction with the notion of reincarnation itself rather than deal with all the undergirding ideas.

## What is reincarnation?

It will be helpful if we begin with a definition. There is no one idea of reincarnation or what is sometimes called "transmigration of souls" or "metempsychosis". Nevertheless, a common denominator of the idea of reincarnation is that our soul or essence is, in some way, passed on after we die and injected into a new body at birth. The *Bhagavad Gita* (part of the Hindu scriptures composed around 300 BC) says: "Just as a person casts off worn-out garments and puts on others that are new, even so does the embodied soul cast off worn-out bodies and take on others that are new" (2:22). Some people say that reincarnation is restricted to humans. Others, who are often vegetarians, claim it involves animals and insects.

Reincarnation could be described as follows. A "soul" enters the physical world as a mineral or single-cell organism and evolves through incarnations (which may even involve lives on other planets) until it attains human status. What is passed from one life to the next and reborn is not the conscious self. Rather, at birth the self comes into existence and ceases at death. However, underlying the series of selves is an eternal, spiritual reality (sometimes called *jiva*) in which a complete memory of the whole series of lives exists. Once it has become human, the soul is generally thought unable to regress to a lower state, even though a soul may endure thousands of lives as a human.

Only through the sufferings endured by humans can sufficient merit be attained to achieve the enlightenment necessary for liberation from the cycle of rebirths. In the period between each death and reincarnation – variously said to be from a few hours to many years – our life principle (sometimes called our *karma*), which reflects the balance of good and evil in our lives, mechanistically determines the kind of birth next appropriate for us. Finally, on enlightenment we transcend self-centredness and become consciously merged into the primordial, universal vacuum called "The Night of Brahma".

## Hinduism and Buddhism

Both Hindus and Buddhists teach reincarnation, though it is more often associated with Hinduism. According to Hindu thought, reincarnation is repeated until the soul reaches its potential in identity with the one infinite and eternal Spirit. For Buddhists, the word "rebirth" is more appropriate to describe their beliefs. The impersonal life-force is believed to be transferred from one life to the next much as a flame passes from one candle to another. This continues, as Professor John Hick (b. 1922) says, until the soul "attains to nirvana by obliterating within itself the needs and drives which have kept the illusion-bound and pain-bearing ego going through life after life."[2]

## Islam

Not all ancient Eastern religions have reincarnation as part of their beliefs. Islam's common roots with Judaism have meant that orthodox Islam disavows reincarnation, taking up the concept of resurrection.

Instead, influenced by Judaism and Christianity, Islam teaches that, after death, faithful Muslims go to heaven, a place of joy and bliss.

## The Celts

The Celts' view of life after death, as known to us from Welsh poetry and Breton folklore, appears to have much in common with some Eastern thought. This is not surprising, as Britain seems to have been in contact with the East from early times. Life was seen as a trial which, if passed, would enable our spirit to rest after death until the moment came for our reincarnation. Reincarnation was repeated until our perfection was attained: admission to Gwenved, the "white" heaven, where we would become fully conscious of God.[3]

## The early history of reincarnation

With life being viewed as a dreary burden in Eastern religions, rebirth is not seen as an opportunity for new life but the experience of recurring hard times for the soul on its journey to perfection and release from existence. However, for Westerners infused with centuries of Judaeo-Christian optimism about the after-life, reincarnation generally takes on positive overtones in that there is the hope that the next reincarnation will be more pleasant and fulfilling than the last.

It is generally claimed that reincarnation is an extremely old belief about life after death. To some extent it is. The Greek historian Herodotus (c. 484–c. 425 BC) thought the ancient Egyptians believed in what we know as the transmigration of souls. But he was mistaken.[4] There is only a marginal mention of something like transmigration in the older section of the *Vedas*, the basic Hindu scriptures written around 1500 BC.

In the West there are traces of the idea of reincarnation in Pythagoras (c. 550–c. 500 BC), but it was not commonly accepted or taken seriously. Plato, who argues for reincarnation on the basis that we are born with opinions which only have to be awakened by questioning to become knowledge (*Meno* 86A–B; *Phaedo* 74A–75E), quotes Socrates who spoke of the ancient doctrine of the transmigration of souls. In the East it is not until around 400 BC when we come to the *Upanishads*, the commentaries on the *Vedas*, that reincarnation becomes central to all Hindu thought. Its fully developed form is found in the semicanonical *Bhagavad Gita*, composed around the fourth century BC (compare 2:22, quoted at the head of this chapter).

## A case for reincarnation

To make a case for reincarnation we would have to argue, first, that our consciousness survives death. That we have already done in chapter 1. Then we would have to argue that after death our life will be in a bodily rather than in a disembodied form. That we will be trying to do in chapter 5. So far, so good. However, thirdly, more specific arguments are needed if we are to believe that our conscious, embodied after-life is to be in the form of reincarnation, rather than, say, resurrection (see chapter 5). It is to these more specific arguments that we now turn, beginning with the moral case that incarnation is what we can expect after we die.

### The moral argument

This is the most important argument for reincarnation; it is an extension of the case for life after death which we set out in chapter 1. The point is put succinctly by an Indian guru, Sri

Chinmoy: "Now if our aim is to enter into the Highest, the Infinite, the Eternal, the Immortal, then naturally one short span of life is not enough."[5] When this argument is filled out by those who believe in reincarnation it is something like this: while some inequalities in life between people come about as the result of decisions we make in life, some are not. That is, our decisions and the way we live our lives cannot account for the different levels of skill, ability or character between people. Rather, such differences are to be accounted for on the basis of our different past lives. The quality of our successive past lives has been recorded by our *karma* or life-force, the resulting balance of good and evil being expressed in the tendency of our present life.

We may grasp this better through an example. Suppose we focus our life – our thoughts, decisions and actions – on acquiring wealth. This attitude is laid up in our *karma*. In attempting to free us from this hankering after wealth, in our next life our *karma* may cause us to be reborn (perhaps a number of successive times) into poverty. Or, we may be born into riches to teach us the hollowness of wealth. (As Oscar Wilde quipped, the only thing worse than not having our desires granted is having them granted.) In this way, through the continuity of our *karma*, our present life can be seen as an expression of our past one.

However, this moral argument has profound and fundamental flaws. The view that *karma* solves the problem of injustices and differences between people in this life is erroneous. There are two basic problems with the idea of karma:

1. Since personalities are obliterated at death, the reincarnated soul is really another person with another person's *karma,* so reincarnation does nothing to solve the inequalities in any one person's life.
2. As we will see, there is no guarantee that, in any one life, good *karma* will increase faster than bad *karma*.

We can take up the example of Adolf Hitler to show how reincarnation is expected to work – or fails to work.[6] We will see that reincarnation does not solve the problem of injustice in the inequalities between people. According to the theory of reincarnation, Hitler would have to be reincarnated many times, some would say in excess of 6 million times, in order to compensate for the total number of victims of his concentration camps. And, in each of Hitler's reincarnations, he would have to suffer in a similar way to those who suffered at his hands. We can suppose that, two years after his death, Hitler is reincarnated as a crippled baby named Edgar Jones, born in New York. But Edgar has no idea that he is the reincarnation of Hitler nor that he is bearing the massive burden of the *karma* debt, and suffering for the crimes of the Nazi Führer. In this example we can see that reincarnation does not provide a solution to the problem of injustices in life. The truth is that Hitler ceased to exist at his death and is not paying his debt, while Edgar is being victimized.

Suppose, further, that when Edgar Jones dies, another person is reincarnated with Hitler's *karma*, and that this cycle is repeated many millions of times. But it is not Hitler who is paying for his sin. Instead, the effects of his sin are multiplied through the further suffering of millions in future reincarnations. Thus, in addition to the original victims of Hitler's regime, there are now many more innocent victims in the reincarnations of Hitler. The tragedy of this scheme is multiplied in that there is no guarantee that Hitler's *karma* could be contained or brought into balance in the successive incarnations. The bitter pill of these painful reincarnations would probably cause a chain-reaction of suffering and bitterness to spread out from those so incarnated, because the bitterness would cause more bad *karma*.

To this injustice must be added a further dimension of innocent suffering in that the vast majority of people are living in ignorance of what is happening to them and are therefore not living in harmony with cosmic truth, producing more bad than good *karma*. As Mark Albrecht is right to conclude: "This is sheer madness, a living hell spreading like a contagious disease . . . [I]n any event his [Hitler's] karma could hardly be contained and might spread infectiously throughout the universe in an eternal nightmare of spiritual bubonic plague."[7] From this we can conclude that the moral case for reincarnation is a travesty of cosmic and personal common justice.

Rather than resort to an idea of what turns out to be morally grotesque, the traditional Christian answer to this particular problem of inequalities in life is to say that, in creating each person *ab initio* (from the beginning), God is responsible for the differences and inequalities between us. Further, not only is God responsible for the unalterable differences and inequalities between us but also this life is not a dreary burden from which to escape (hopefully) to higher forms of reincarnated life. Though "joy and woe are woven fine", as William Blake (1757–1827) put it, life on earth is, at least for the Christian, a rich experience of growing in understanding and in a relationship with God. This growing relationship is not an automatic process, however. It is a life of choosing to respond to God's love in the way we live in loving him and others.

Further, Christians hold the view that this life is not too short but quite adequate in providing opportunities to develop a positive relationship with God (Ephesians 2:1–10). Also, if we allow God's Spirit to control our lives, this life is not inadequate to develop a present life increasingly characterized by, for example, love, joy, peace, patience, kindness, generosity, faithfulness, gentleness and self-control (compare Galatians 5:22).

*The argument from twins*

Along the same lines as the moral argument, those making a case for reincarnation will point to unexpected dissimilarities between identical twins, or geniuses or child prodigies in families of otherwise ordinary children. These differences, it is suggested, are more reasonably accounted for if we assume the results of a previous life are being expressed rather than suppose environmental or hereditary factors are at work. However, those already sceptical of the notion of reincarnation from a moral point of view would maintain that a more thorough exploration of hereditary and environmental factors is likely to provide an adequate account of such differences.

## Empirical evidence?

We can now turn to seek what is said to be more empirical evidence for reincarnation, evidence which is offered in abundance and in two kinds. One kind of evidence collected from "hypnotic regression" comes from, for example, Dr Helen Wambach of San Francisco. She describes her method of research in which over 2,000 subjects were involved. Like other past-life hypnotherapists, she enlists volunteers for group sessions. Under hypnosis she asks subjects to go back, say, to the year 1800 and describe their impressions. If there is no response she tries another date. Or, she may use the "world tour" technique in which she tells those in the group that they are going to float all around the world, back into past time. When she calls out a place name, the participants are encouraged to let images come to mind.[8]

The material produced by this method is considerable and of varying interest. One difficulty arises from Wambach's admission that she did not check all 1,088 data sheets for factual and historical discrepancies. Another difficulty is that she has not recognized the elementary problem that she and her clients are using "BC" dating terminology for times when people did not have such a concept of living before Christ. In any case, Wambach admits that her hypnotic sessions are an effective means of therapy rather than proof of the historical reality of reincarnation. Indeed, in attempting to explain what is happening she has also speculated that the brain is like a receiver tuning in to what "is".[9]

However, most psychologists are sceptical about the value of such therapies to support the idea of the existence of past lives. An example comes from Alexander Rogawski, former chief of the Los Angeles County Medical Association's psychiatry section. He said rather bluntly that all that the therapy's popularity proves is that "suckers are born every minute and customers can be found for everything."[10] Professor Ernest Hilgard, director of the Hypnosis Research Laboratory at Stanford University, is equally scathing of hypnotic recall:

> Hypnosis is a very dangerous tool best used by formally trained people. New identities claimed during trance are not uncommon and very easy to produce. Invariably, they're related to long buried memories, and anybody who makes claims to the contrary has not based them on scholarly judgments.[11]

In Britain, psychiatrist Anthony Storr argues that hypnotic recall is an example of cryptoamnesia, a fantasy based on subconscious recollections of some long-forgotten story we have read, or information we have obtained.[12] For example, Ruth Simmons, a Colorado housewife, claimed to have lived previously as Bridey Murphy in 19th century Ireland. However, it was shown that "Bridey" gained all her knowledge of her "past life" consciously and unconsciously through her Irish nanny.[13] A large proportion of so-called "past life" recall is probably accounted for by cryptoamnesia.

Another kind of evidence claimed to support reincarnation is "spontaneous recall". For this, the research of Dr Ian Stevenson from the University of Virginia is well known. Typically, in relation to his research, a child usually between the ages of two and four begins to show signs of personality changes. Soon the child insists he or she is another person who has lived and recently died in the surrounding area. Stevenson then interviews the child and checks the details of the reported memories with the family of the deceased person. Stevenson prefers to interview children because of the greater difficulty of controlling subconscious influences in adults. In 90% of the cases (which he has researched in detail) he has found that claims to knowledge – of names and foreign languages, locations, skills, events, and objects kept in locations unknown to others – are remarkably accurate.[14]

Stevenson's careful methodology has not been faulted by his peers.[15] While he does not disclose his own beliefs, and he claims neither to believe or disbelieve in reincarnation, looking back on his research Stevenson said, in an interview in 1974: "What I do believe is that, of the cases we now know, reincarnation – at least for some – is the best explanation that we have been able to come up with." Then he said, "I think a rational person, if he wants, can believe in reincarnation on the basis of evidence."[16]

Skeptics may quickly point to the many reports that have been exposed as "fakes". However, even if we set these aside, there remain four comments which can be made in relation to Stevenson's work that reduce its value for supporting the notion of reincarnation.

First, a question must be raised about the motive of those thousands of people who report their cases to Stevenson, a known reincarnation researcher – for this indicates at least their partial interest towards the belief. This point is strengthened when we note that there is an average gap of three to five years between the first supposed symptoms of a previous life and it being made public, during which time subtle or overt reinforcement of the reality of a past life may take place.

Secondly and relatedly, as Stevenson admits, in the general cultural milieu of his examples there is a consensus of belief in reincarnation; that is, American cases are much weaker in details and less frequent in occurrences than cases in Asia, where reincarnation is a common aspect of belief systems.[17]

Thirdly, past life recall could result from the spirit of a dead person or even by demonic possession. For example, Stevenson reports that in the spring of 1954 Jasbir, a three-year-old Indian boy, became ill with smallpox.[18] He lapsed into a coma which his parents mistook temporarily for death. Hours later he recovered. A few weeks later Jasbir displayed a remarkable transformation of behaviour. He claimed to be a brahmin named Sobha Ram, from a nearby village, who had died in an accident at the age of 22 on 22 May 1954. While this case displayed all the normal features of spontaneous recall, it was not reincarnation, for the boy was three years old when Sobha died. Rather, this was probably a case of possession, either by the dead man's spirit or some spirit impersonating him. This view is given credence in that the voice of the dead man spoke through Jasbir.

Fourthly, as Stevenson also admits, there is the strong possibility of a paranormal or psychic explanation behind these reports recalling past lives.[19] There is, among some fields of science, an attempt to uncover the existence of a sensory perception beyond our presently known five senses. Thus, in the future it may be possible to show that past life recall is the result of extra-sensory perception (ESP), or clairvoyance, or telepathic communication. At the very least, we can say that, until we know more about the workings of the human mind as well as the spiritual world, it is premature to use Stevenson's research as evidence of reincarnation.

## More problems with reincarnation

So far, we have been examining the case for reincarnation and found it sorely wanting, especially from a moral perspective. Before turning to see what support may be gained for reincarnation from the Bible and the early church, there are some other objections to reincarnation we need to take into account.

### Reincarnation and the "sound of silence"

As is commonly known, the purpose of reincarnation is to work off all bad *karma* until the "sound of silence" – the primordial state of the universe – is recaptured. But this assumption that good *karma* is increasing is unfounded. Since the collapse of confidence in modernism and the disillusionment with the hope of the Enlightenment that society is evolving into an ever better environment for people, few if any would agree that we, or our society as a whole, are improving. In India, for example, where reincarnation has been taught most thoroughly for the longest time, it is difficult to conclude that society is improving. Indeed, we have already seen that the notion of reincarnation is beset with the problem not of increasing good, but of how the syndrome of rapidly multiplying bad *karma* can be reversed.

### The meaninglessness of life

The doctrine of reincarnation includes the important idea that at death one's personality is obliterated. The implication of this is that personality is taken to be of little significance, for, according to the doctrine of reincarnation, all personalities are ultimately interchangeable or even eventually synonymous, with everyone seemingly suffering for everyone and everything. For many people this raises the question of how life can possibly be meaningful. In our lives, everything that we hope for is bound up with our personal existence. If our personal, distinct existence is not only uncertain but ends at death, we have no hope nor is there meaning in this life. From this perspective, in thinking about life after death, we are no better off than the atheist – perhaps worse off.

### The injustice of "dharma"

The concept of *dharma* involves the inevitability of what must be, or "doing what is set before you". This is at the base of the Indian saying that, "It is the *dharma* of fire to burn". This notion of *dharma* has two important consequences. On the one hand, it leads to the view that nothing is urgent since the cosmic *dharma* of life is unfolding in a way predetermined by one's *karma*. In any case, there is always another chance – at least for one's *karma* if not for us – so that moral choices are less important than they would otherwise be. On the other hand, the *dharma* aspect of reincarnation is that there is a cosmic necessity in even the most tragic events. For example, John-Roger Hinkins, a Los Angeles "spiritual leader" and head of the "Movement of Spiritual Inner Awareness", had this to say about the Vietnam war:

> There was no overkill; there was no underkill. The Americans that went over there and were caught up in it were part of the Vietnamese process thousands of years ago, and even though they were born in America this life, they were pulled back there to complete their karma, also. And those who went through the war unharmed were not part of the process and came home safely. So how can that action be judged "wrong"?[20]

On this reading, the Vietnam war was a cosmic necessity, as were such other tragedies as the Holocaust, the 1945 bombing of Dresden and the reigns of Joseph Stalin and Idi Amin. Thoughtful people can only respond to such twisted reasoning with a cry of "No!". Christians will want to point to the love of the Creator God who wants to rescue us from what is no less than tragic and gross sin.

## Reincarnation in the Bible?

As much as it may surprise traditional Christians, the Bible is sometimes said to contain or support a belief in reincarnation.[21] Four passages in particular – all from the New Testament – have been brought into view to show that the Bible teaches reincarnation. However, while reincarnation could well have

been part of the thought world of first-century people represented in the Bible, on a closer examination, the doctrine is
certainly not taught in the Bible.

The first passage that is supposedly about reincarnation is
Mark 9:11–13. It is a discussion between Jesus and Peter,
James and John about the return of Elijah. The supposed ref-
erence to reincarnation is Jesus saying that Elijah has come
back. However, Jesus is referring cryptically to John the
Baptist, and John the Baptist is not a reincarnation of Elijah.
Rather, in the pattern of classic biblical typology, John the
Baptist is a "type" of Elijah, fulfilling the role of Elijah "with
the spirit and power of Elijah", as it is put in Luke 1:17.

A second scripture that could be taken as teaching or
implying a doctrine of reincarnation is John 3:3. In debate
with a Pharisee named Nicodemus, Jesus is reported as saying, "no one can see the kingdom of God without being born
again" (John 3:3, my translation). What may seem like support for reincarnation quickly evaporates when we note that
the Greek word for "again" is *anōthen*. This word has a
double meaning: "again" and "above". Far from teaching
reincarnation, the double meaning of this word is used to give
rise to Nicodemus misunderstanding Jesus and to propel the
dialogue forward. The ensuing dialogue makes it plain that
*anōthen* is to be taken to mean "above", for Jesus goes on to
say that the second birth is to be a spiritual one experienced
by a person in this life, in order to see God's powerful reign.

Thirdly, John 9:1–3 is clearer. John says that as Jesus was
walking along he saw a man born blind. Jesus' disciples asked
him who had sinned, the man or his parents, that he was born
blind. It seems clear that the disciples are assumed to be enter-
taining a number of views: sickness can be a punishment for
sin; punishment for sin can be transmitted from one generation to another; the man may have sinned during a previous
life. Jesus' answer is a direct rebuttal of any ideas that
sickness is a punishment for sin or that punishment can be

transmitted (compare Jeremiah 31:30–31). Jesus says, "Neither this man nor his parents sinned" (John 9:3). For the doctrine of reincarnation there is neither rebuttal nor support.

Fourthly, James 3:6 says that the tongue sets on fire "the cycle of nature", or "the wheel of birth". The idea of a cycle of becoming and passing away was used in early Greek literature associated with the mythical figure Orpheus.[22] But over its long history, and in the various words that were used, the phrase became a general saying that could include the meaning of "the whole course of life", as it does here. Again there is no support for reincarnation.

From this glance at four passages that are said to teach reincarnation we can see that it is misguided to find support in the Bible for such views. We can also recall from the last chapter that Old Testament writers largely avoided speculating about life after death. More specifically, we have to keep in mind the biblical passages which implicitly deny any notion of reincarnation. For example, in the Old Testament, 2 Samuel 14:14 says: "We must all die; we are like water spilled on the ground, which cannot be gathered up." And in Philippians 1:23 Paul's assumption and desire is that when he dies he will be with Christ rather than, say, be reincarnated.[23]

## A censored Bible?

The idea that the Bible once contained teaching on reincarnation which the church eliminated in the sixth and later centuries[24] is a case without any supporting evidence, for the present text of the whole Bible is well attested as early as the second century. There is absolutely no evidence that the text of the Bible was reworked before that, in order to eliminate any teaching on reincarnation.

The Bible could be taken to contain echoes of the ideas of reincarnation found at the time (John 9:2). However, not only is the doctrine nowhere supported, it is explicitly without support at a crucial point (John 9:1–3), and in other biblical passages it is denied (see note 23). We can conclude that re-incarnation has no part in a Christianity that takes the Bible as its test of orthodoxy. But this is not the end of the matter for some people.

## Reincarnation in the early church?

Not only is it suggested that material in the Bible which taught reincarnation has been repressed. It is also alleged that some early church fathers taught reincarnation and that their views were likewise condemned and their writings removed from history.[25]

It is true that the Egyptian biblical scholar and theologian Origen (c. 185–c. 254 AD), who founded a theological school in Caesarea, taught that souls pre-existed. He said that, before entering a human body, souls were angelic beings whose good or evil deeds determined birth on earth. But in the year 553 AD, the Council of Constantinople condemned Origen's teaching on the pre-existence of souls. However, Origen specifically denied the transmigration of souls. That is, he denied that souls moved from one body to another after their initial incarnation of the soul. For example, when discussing the relation of John the Baptist to Elijah (Matthew 17:10, see above) he says that he does not want to "fall into the dogma of transmigration, which is foreign to the church of God, and not handed down by the Apostles, nor anywhere set forth in the Scripture."[26]

In any case, at no council in the first thousand years of the church's history was a move ever made against reincarnation, for the simple reason that it was never taught by any of the church fathers. For example, in his *Dialogue with Trypho* Justin Martyr (c. 100–c. 165), an early Christian apologist, agreed with his opponent Trypho the Jew that "souls neither see God nor transmigrate into other bodies" (chapter 4). Tertullian (c. 160–c. 220 AD), an African church father, who took some space to refute the doctrine of transmigration, said it was "a falsehood, which was not only shameful, but also hazardous." He said it was indeed manifest that dead men are formed from living ones, but that it did not follow from that, that living men are formed from dead ones. He also raised the customary objection that the idea of reincarnation is not consistent with the increase in the population of the world, but with the possibility of other inhabited planets this objection does not have the force it once had (*On the Soul* 28–35).

We can allow Gregory of Nyssa to sum up early church thinking. As noted earlier in this chapter, he thought that ideas of reincarnation were "really fitting for the chatter of frogs or jackdaws, the stupidity of fishes, or the insensibility of trees."[27] This strong repudiation of reincarnation is not only because early Christianity arose out of Judaism, which placed a high value on individuals and their relationship with God in this and the next life, but also because the early church took its cue from the resurrection of Jesus for their understanding of the after-life.

## In sum . . .

For those who wrote the New Testament, and for those who followed them, the idea of reincarnation was in the air they breathed. However, the doctrine is nowhere supported, but rather it is denied in the Bible.

If we have correctly described the idea of reincarnation, we are left with a doctrine that has four profound inadequacies.[28]

First, reincarnation is a misnomer for what is believed. The individual personality is not reincarnated but extinguished at death, a fate no different from that assumed by the atheist. What is said to live beyond death is our *karma,* which is reincarnated in a completely different personality without memory or knowledge of the past – hardly a meaningful life after death.

Secondly, reincarnation does not eliminate evil. Contrary to the belief that reincarnation allows evil *karma* to be balanced in successive reincarnations, it is foisted upon innocent victims who, without any mechanism to control their response to it, are destined to perpetuate the tragic weight of the past. Further, there is no guarantee in what is seen to be a capricious universe that a good man will not be reincarnated as a deadly snake, or as a saint, or a thief.

Thirdly, the idea of reincarnation is not proved by past-life recall. All reports of so-called memories of a past life can be more reasonably accounted for by such suggestions as mediumship, seances, spirit contact, demon possession, psychic trance utterances or cryptoamnesia. This is supported by a telling open letter from the orthodox Hindu swami Sri Sri Somasundara Desika Paramachariya of south India to Ian Stevenson. The Hindu swami accepts the traditional Hindu doctrine of reincarnation. The pertinent lines read: "All 300 odd cases reported by you do not in fact support the theory of reincarnation . . . They are all spirit possessions, ignored by the learned in south India."[29]

We can see that there may be nothing intrinsically impossible about reincarnation; in tackling this issue we need to avoid a simplistic condemnation. But our discussion has left us with such large questions about its logical and moral problems that, if we are going to think clearly about life after death, it will not be through following or developing the idea of reincarnation. In any case, we can conclude that reincarnation has no part in a Christianity that takes the Bible as its test of orthodoxy. The Bible, as well as the early church, specifically condemned the doctrine. We cannot unthinkingly blend reincarnation into Christianity. We will, therefore, turn now to consider another option.

## Notes

[1] Cited by Mark C. Albrecht, *Reincarnation: A Christian Critique of a New Age Doctrine* (Downers Grove: IVP, 1982), p. 11.

[2] John Hick, *Death and Eternal Life* (Louisville, KY: Westminster/John Knox, 1994), p. 28.

[3] Winifred Bryher, *Ruan: A Novel* (London: Collins, 1961), pp. 8–9.

[4] James Henry Breasted, *Development of Religion and Thought in Ancient Egypt* (London: Hodder & Stoughton, 1912), p. 277.

[5] Cited by Albrecht, *Reincarnation*, p. 82.

[6] For what follows see Albrecht, *Reincarnation*, pp. 90–91.

[7] Albrecht, *Reincarnation*, p. 91.

[8] Helen Wambach, *Reliving Past Lives: The Evidence Under Hypnosis* (London: Hutchinson, 1979).

[9] Albrecht, *Reincarnation*, pp. 53–56.

[10] "Where Were You in 1643?: Therapy for the Born-Again", *Time* (Sydney, 3 October 1977), p. 67.

[11] Cited by Albrecht, *Reincarnation*, pp. 68–69.

[12] *Time* (Sydney, 3 October 1977), p. 53 cited by Albrecht, *Reincarnation*, p. 69.

[13] See Renée Haynes, "Reincarnation – Objections and Alternatives", *Christian Parapsychologist* 3 (4, 1979), p. 136.

[14] See J. Gaither Pratt and Naomi Hintze, *The Psychic Realm: What Can You Believe?* (New York: Random House, 1975) quoted in Sylvia Cranston and Carey Williams, *Reincarnation: A New Horizon in Science, Religion and Society* (New York: Julian, 1984), pp. 49–68.

[15] Compare, for example, Harold I. Lief, "Commentary on Dr. Ian Stevenson's 'The Evidence of Man's Survival after Death'", *Journal of Nervous and Mental Disease* 165 (3, 1977), pp. 171–73.

[16] Quoted by Alton Slagle, "Reincarnation: A Doctor Looks

Beyond Death", *Sunday News*, (New York, 4 August 1974), from Cranston and Williams, *Reincarnation*, p. 68.

[17] Ian Stevenson, "Have You Lived Before?" *Family Circle* (14 June, 1978), p. 39 cited by, for example, Albrecht, *Reincarnation*, p. 59.

[18] Ian Stevenson, *Twenty Cases Suggestive of Reincarnation* (Charlottesville, VA: University Press of Virginia, 1974), pp. 34–52.

[19] See Cranston and Williams, *Reincarnation*, pp. 57–62.

[20] Cited by Albrecht, *Reincarnation*, p. 103–104 from *The Movement Newspaper* (August, 1980), pp. 22–23.

[21] Compare Marilyn Grace Graham, *On Reincarnation: The Gospel According to Paul: An Interpretive Matrix Explaining Romans* (Miami: Quest, 1998).

[22] See the literature cited by Martin Dibelius, *James* (Philadelphia: Fortress, 1976), pp. 196–97 n. 79.

[23] See also 2 Samuel 12:23; Psalm 78:39; Luke 23:39–43; Acts 17:31; 2 Corinthians 5:1, 4, 8; 6:2; Galatians 2:16; 3:10–13; Ephesians 2:8–9; Hebrews 9:27; 10:12–14; Revelation 20:11–15.

[24] Joseph Head and S. L. Cranston, *Reincarnation: The Phoenix Fire Mystery* (New York: Crown, 1977), p. 134.

[25] So Leoline L. Wright, *Reincarnation* (San Diego: Point Loma, 1975), p. 67; Anna Kennedy Winner, *The Basic Ideas of Occult Wisdom* (London: Theosophical Publishing, 1970), p. 56.

[26] Origen, *Matthew* 13:1; compare Origen, *Contra Celsum* 1:20; 3:75; 6:36.

[27] Gregory of Nyssa, *On the Making of Man* 28:3.

[28] See also Albrecht, *Reincarnation*, pp. 127–30.

[29] Quoted in Lynn de Silva, *Reincarnation in Buddhist and Christian Thought* (Colombo, Sri Lanka: Christian Literature Society of Ceylon, 1968), p. 49, cited by Albrecht, *Reincarnation*, p. 129.

# 4

## Do We Have an Immortal Soul?

If we are going to live after we die, what is it about us that is going to survive death? Some would say we have an immortal soul that lives on after we die. This is obvious, it is said; we naturally think of ourselves as having two parts – a body (including our brain) which contains our soul. Great thinkers like Plato would agree, and have thought that our soul is our most important part. Others, like Aristotle (and most famously, René Descartes), took the view that we are only human because we have both a body and a soul. Thus both our body and our soul must survive death. But, in more recent times this idea has been ridiculed as "the Ghost in the Machine" theory. Instead, the view has developed that it is our working brain that is actually what we imagine to be our soul.

Yet, some of the great thinkers of our time are making a convincing case that we have an immortal soul. If we are to hold this view we would have to explain how we are going to live without a body. Despite what seems to be the inevitable course of this chapter, we are caught off balance when we turn to the Bible. In the Bible we are surprised – perhaps disturbed – when we ask the question as to whether or not we have a soul which lives on after we die.

# Do We Have an Immortal Soul?

"Is there a 'Ghost in the Machine'?"
Gilbert Ryle

"O God (if there is a God),
save my soul (if I have a soul)"
Agnostic's prayer

If we were to ask those who believe in some kind of life after death, what form they expect it to take, the answer would probably be that our soul, or perhaps our mind, spirit or personality, continues to live on after our death. However, some people who have been influenced by the philosophical fashions of the first half of the 20th century would tell us that our inner life consists of nothing more than our brain and its processes. Thus, once we are dead, without brain power, there is no chance of life after death. In an increasingly secular society this view is gaining popularity. So we need to begin this chapter on the soul and our after-life with a fundamental question.

## Is our soul only the processes of our brain?

A serious assault on the view that we have a spiritual or non-material and non-locatable inner part of us called a soul, which uses our brain as an instrument for our thought, comes from those who want to identify our mind or soul with our brain. Many distinguished thinkers hold or have held some form of this so-called "identity theory". Francis Crick (b. 1916), the discoverer of DNA and one of the winners of the

1962 Nobel prize in physiology or medicine, and Willard Van Orman Quine (1908–2000), the most influential American philosopher of the last half of the 20th century, as well as Richard Rorty (b. 1931), that much-talked-about American postmodern philosopher, are examples. They tell us that our inner experiences are simply processes of our brain's activity. While the ascendency of this view is quite recent, the English philosopher Thomas Hobbes (1588–1679) most famously championed this idea. He argued that since actions of our bodies can only be caused by other bodily actions, what happens in our minds must be of a physical nature. This means, given the right tools and conditions, that what we experience in our inner selves could be observed by a neurologist.

But, according to equally distinguished thinkers – notably René Descartes (see below), Sir John Eccles (1903–97), a winner of the Nobel prize for physiology or medicine in 1963, and Wilder Penfield (1891–1976) the American neurosurgeon, for example – this theory does not stand up to the scrutiny of our experience. We know that thoughts are not the same as our brain, for a medical specialist may examine our brain, but the specialist is not seeing thoughts. Also, if our mind or soul was no more than the chemical changes in our brain we would have no genuine freedom of thought. That is, with sufficient knowledge of our brain, someone could predict everything we did because we would be acting simply in response to chemical changes in our brain. But this does not seem to accord with our experience where our thoughts and intentions are involved. For example, I know the difference between an automatic action (a spasm or tick) and a voluntary action (typing on this laptop or tapping my foot to music in the background) in which there is something else happening in my inner self between my mind and my actions. Thus, if we can weigh and decide between thoughts and actions, we must be more than a physical brain.

Despite these criticisms, supporters of the "identity theory" would not be convinced. Surely, they would say, even a mechanically determined brain could stop one thought and begin another to assess the previous thought or action. Indeed, some time in the future, it may be discovered that, in splitting the brain into its hemispheres, each half possesses its own consciousness. This would mean that the brain was the mind and that we do not have a mind or soul separately acting on the brain. But this is pure speculation.

However, there is a refined version of the view that we have a mind (or soul) as well as a brain. This view says that, in such activities as rational thought – scientific inquiry with its purposive activity and subsequent conscious reflection, as well as our responsible decision-making – we show ourselves to be free to make choices. Those who argue in this way say that these activities would be impossible if our brain and mind (or soul) were one and the same thing – simply obeying the laws of physics and chemistry.

Nevertheless, this discussion (which is much more subtle and complex than we have been able to show) has left us with such uncertainty that we will need to take another way forward in discovering whether or not we have a soul or mind separate from our body.

## Do we have an immortal soul?

Most people would say that it is obvious we have a soul, because from our experience we naturally think of ourselves as having at least two parts: a body (including our brain), which contains or embodies our non-physical part. This supposed non-physical part of our life is described by a range of terms: mind, spirit, ego, superego, psyche, consciousness, I, person, id, mentality, our subconscious or unconscious, or soul, for example.

## Plato

Even after more than 2,000 years, the thinking of Plato (c. 429–347 BC) is still influential in the way we think about the possibility of our having a soul. Plato's demonstration that we have a soul is based on the idea of movement or change and growth. He argues that movement and change in our lives points to something that must be in itself movement and change, as well as able to cause the motion and growth. This is the soul, the very essence of self-motion, the principle and energy of life. According to Plato, God created both the world soul as well as human souls out of the same ingredients. Plato warns that his account is a myth and is also happy to say that the soul is without a beginning.[1]

For Plato, our soul is our most valuable possession and its condition our greatest concern. Our soul is prior to, superior to, ruler of, and distinct from our body, yet our body and soul interact with each other. That our soul is immortal Plato thought clear for a number of reasons. However, to our post-modern minds these appear somewhat quaint and inadequate. For example, he thought that life follows death because of the eternal cycle of opposites or contraries such as sleeping and waking, and life and death. Also, since the soul rules the body it functions like the divine. So, like the divine, it must be unchanging and immortal. Another of Plato's arguments for the immortality of our soul runs as follows. Things are destroyed through some inherent evil in them. The evils of the soul are unrighteousness, intemperance, cowardice and ignorance. However, since a good and a bad person can live equally short or long lives the soul is, therefore, not destroyed by external evil; it must, in turn therefore, be immortal.[2]

From Plato onwards, the idea that each of us is an embodied spirit or soul (and therefore we are by nature immortal) has had an illustrious history, this idea generally being taken up by the early church. Saint Augustine (354–430 AD), for example, picking up Plato's idea of eternal cycles of opposites or contraries such as death and life, also argued that our soul is immortal. For him, the relationship between our bodies and our souls is explained by saying that our soul uses our body. But in order to prevent our thinking that our soul is immortal by itself (without reference to God), he said that our souls participate in life and, therefore, cannot die.

## Aristotle

Another celebrated ancient philosopher, Aristotle (384–322 BC), took a slightly different view of the soul. His views are also important because they too have gained appeal. In *De Anima* he said that the purpose of psychology is "to discover the nature and essence of soul, and its attributes" (402a7). He explained that the soul is the vital principle or life-force which endows life and – in higher forms of the soul – gives movement to living things. The lowest form of soul is the nutritive or vegetative soul found in plants. Animals have a slightly higher form of soul, for they have the powers of sense-perception (which leads to imagination and memory), desire and movement. Our higher human soul includes all these powers and also gives us the abilities of a mind: the ability to pursue truth and solve problems. This part of our soul, which is the mind, not only pre-exists us but is immortal. Yet the soul is not imprisoned in our bodies; it needs to be united with the body to perform its functions.

At this point Aristotle is quite different from Plato. We could say that Plato argued that we are a soul in a body: Aristotle argued that we are an inseparable single entity formed by our body and our soul.

Aristotle's view is important, for it was the view generally taken up by the early church. For example, Irenaeus (c. 130–c. 200), the bishop of Lyon, said that the soul and the spirit are part of the human being but they are not what constitutes a person. Following in the tradition of Aristotle – yet adding his

Christian perspective about the involvement of the Spirit – he said that "the perfect man consists in the comingling and the union of the soul receiving the spirit of the Father, and the admixture of that fleshly nature which was moulded after the image of God" (*Against Heresies* 5:6:1). Succinctly, Saint Cyril (c. 315–387), bishop of Jerusalem, put it to his hearers in a lecture: "that as a man you are of a twofold nature, consisting of a soul and a body" (*Lecture* 4:18).

## Thomas Aquinas and John Calvin

This twofold nature of a human being was also a part of the belief system of Saint Thomas Aquinas (c.1225–74), the Italian philosopher and doctor of the church. In his dependence on Aristotle, Aquinas maintained the immortality of our soul by arguing that our soul is spiritual and much more than a part of us that gives life to our bodies. That is, our soul is not exhausted by its role in our bodies. And he said that our natural desire for immortality, implanted in us by the Author of nature, cannot be in vain. Instead, it is proof that our soul is immortal.

John Calvin (1509–64), the French Protestant reformer, was more Platonic in his view of the soul. Taking his cue from Job 4:19 (where a person is described as living in a house of clay), Calvin says our created soul lives in our body as in a house, not only so that it can animate us but also – even in our sinful state – to enable us to honour God. For Calvin, like Aquinas, our aspiration to immortality points to the immortality of our soul; so also does our knowledge of God and our ability to discern between good and evil (*Institutes of the Christian Religion* 1.15.2, 6).

## René Descartes

So-called modern thinkers, most famously René Descartes (1596–1650), have also been convinced of our being distinctly both a body as well as a soul. Descartes' "substance dualism" is still seen to be important in trying to argue that we have a soul as well as a body. In his *Discourse on the Method* his line of argument went like this: the only thing I can be confident about is that I can think; I cannot even be sure that I have a body; that could be a dream. That means my body is separate from what is truly me, my soul. In a frequently quoted statement which is easily understood (if read slowly!), Descartes put it like this:

> I attentively examined what I was and as I observed that I could suppose that I had no body, and that there was no world nor any place in which I might be; but that I could not therefore suppose that I was not; and that, on the contrary, from the very circumstance that I thought to doubt of the truth of other things, it most clearly and certainly followed that I was; while, on the other hand, if I had only ceased to think, although all the other objects which I had ever imagined had been in reality existent, I would have had no reason to believe that I existed; I thence concluded that I was a substance whose whole essence or nature consists only in thinking, and which, that it may exist, has need of no place, nor is dependent on any material thing; so that "I", that is to say, the mind by which I am what I am, is wholly distinct from the body (part 4).

But you may (and others certainly will) object to the idea that just because I cannot be sure that my body exists it must, therefore, be separate from what is truly me. It could be that I do not know what makes me who I am!

Nevertheless, to follow the thinking of Professor Richard Swinburne of Oxford (b. 1934), if we rework what Descartes said, we may come up with a more convincing argument that we have a soul separate from our body. In bare outline we can put it like this:

- At present I exist as a thinker.
- It is possible (at least logically) that I could go on thinking

and existing even if my body did not continue. (We can say this because – as we will see below – we can imagine and explain what it would be like to live without our body.)

● But it is not obviously possible for me to continue to live unless something of me continues to live.

● Therefore, I must already have another part of me other than my body, that is, my soul.[3]

## David Hume and Immanuel Kant

In spite of the distinguished history of this idea that we have an independent and immortal soul, the view has come under repeated attack, not only, as we have seen, in the "identity theory" discussion. It has also come under siege from philosophers known as empiricists (those who say that our knowledge can come only from our experience). For example, the Scottish philosopher and historian David Hume (1711–76) reduced our inner selves to a series of fleeting impressions or ideas. From his perspective, we are no more than a stream of sensory events. As he said in his *Treatise on Human Nature*, when he entered "into what I call *myself*, I always stumble on some particular perception or other, of heat or cold, light or shade, love or hatred, pain or pleasure. I never catch *myself* at any time without a perception, and never can observe any thing but the perception" (1:4:6, his emphasis). He concluded from this that our minds must consist only of a succession of perceptions. There is no soul inside us.

However, Immanuel Kant claimed to have answered Hume and upheld the view that we have a soul. Kant took the line that for us to understand the relationship between various things in our world we have to be separate from each of them. This anticipates Søren Kierkegaard (1813–55) from Denmark who wrote that, "Man is a synthesis of the psychical and the physical; however, a synthesis is unthinkable if the two are not united in a third. This third is spirit."[4] But this was by no means the end of the debate.

## A "Ghost in the Machine"?

In modern times, the most notable attack on the idea of us having a soul has come from Gilbert Ryle (1900–76) of Oxford in his famous work *The Concept of Mind* (London: Hutchinson, 1949). Since Descartes assumed an unreal or unnatural distinction between our thinking about something and then doing it, Ryle ridiculed Descartes' theory of our physical body being inhabited and "operated" by a mind or soul. He called this the "dogma of the Ghost in the Machine" theory (pp. 15–16). Instead of us having an "inner-man" or a distinct soul, Ryle reduced our inner lives to our dispositions: being generous, or bad tempered, as well as having dispositions of beliefs about things, for example.

But this will not do. We know we have mental processes apart from what we are or do. Take the example of feeling pain. I may cry out or clutch the area of my body where I feel pain. But this is not "the pain", which I know to be separate from me and my response to it. We will add to this point in a moment.

## The soul and ESP

In the ebb and flow of the argument for the existence of a soul as part of our inner life, the balance of the case probably rests with Plato, Descartes and their successors such as Richard Swinburne. To strengthen the case for our having a soul, as well as a physical brain, there may be supporting evidence in extra-sensory perception (ESP). As we noted in the last chapter, ESP is an umbrella term covering a number of supposed mental faculties such as telepathy, clairvoyance and precognition, which are said to allow a person to gain information without using the five senses. If any one of these faculties could be shown to be a reality it would mean that our mind (or part of it) could roam around independent of our body. In turn this would demonstrate that there was a non-material part to our inner selves.

In the mid- to late-20th century there was promise in some quarters that research into the paranormal was yielding results. But closer scrutiny of the work of the ESP researchers has undermined our confidence, so that we can no longer rely upon ESP to help establish whether or not we also have a soul or mind independent of our brains and material bodies.

## The soul and religious experience

If ESP turns out to be an uncertain ally in our pursuit of the soul, we may be given more hope in turning to religious experience. It is true that a great deal of our religious experience comes as a result of our considering the beauty of the natural world or from listening to or participating in music (often associated with worship), as well as from our listening to talks or reading books about religion.

However, there is another aspect of religious experience. It is the kind of religious experience where God is known to us directly. That is, we experience God without our intellect or senses helping or even being involved. With this in mind, the Italian Franciscan theologian and mystic Saint Bonaventure (1221–74) wrote that "God is most truly present to the soul and immediately knowable." This is possible support for our having a soul or mind as well as a brain because it shows that God is communicating with us apart from our brain – that is, to our soul.[5] However, we have to concede that it could be that God is communicating with our brain.[6]

## Choices of the soul

Further support for our having a soul as well as a mind comes from considering the way we can distinguish between truth and falsehood, love and hate, the valuable and the trivial, beauty and beastliness. We are able to choose to help or hinder another person, to act for our own good or for the good of another, even at our expense. In short we are able to make choices other than rational ones determined by the so-called laws of nature. In these decisions and actions our mind is being determined by more than laws of physics and chemistry. Despite Gilbert Ryle's jest, there must be a "Ghost in the Machine".[7]

But our soul – this so-called "Ghost in the Machine" of our body – is not to be imagined as some independent aspect of our inner life that is unaffected by what happens to the rest of our life. What happens in daily life to our body, or to our mind or our soul (in its choices and interaction with God) has an impact on each of the other aspects of our life and being. For example, where we live, falling in love, a religious experience in which we encounter God, being injured, the books we read, each have their impact not on parts but on the whole of our lives – body, mind and soul.

## When and how do we get a soul?

If our soul is that aspect of our inner life that determines the moral choices we make, then it must come into existence after the earliest brain activity (and hence consciousness), which takes place about 42 days after conception. If, following Bonaventure, our soul is that aspect of our inner life which is most immediately sensitive to the knowledge and experience of God, we can speculate (for speculation is all it can be) that our soul comes into existence as (or at the point where) God begins to relate to our consciousness, as it reaches out for meaning and understanding.

If the concept of life after death means that we, as our soul, live on without our body, such a concept of life without a body must be imaginable. To this issue we now turn, in part, in the hope of clarifying whether or not we will live after death as disembodied souls or minds, or whether we need a body (at least of some kind) in the after-life.

## Living without a body

Amazingly, despite the long history of the idea that after we die we will live as disembodied souls or spirits, little thought has been given as to how this might work or what it would be like to live this way. The most famous theory was described in 1953 by the Oxford philosopher H. H. Price (1899–1984) in his long essay, "Personal Survival and the Idea of Another World".

Price sets out to give a plausible picture of our life after death. First, he suggests we will experience life after death in much the same way as we experience dreams in this life. In other words, the ideas and images of our life after death will be supplied by what we have experienced in this life. And our life after death will be experienced as real, and solid, and bodily. However, a supposed major difference between this and the after-life – just as there is a difference between our present life and our dream life – will be that we may experience discontinuities and compressions and transformations. The reason for this suggestion is that we can expect the future life to be governed, not by the laws of physics but by the laws of psychology, which we will explain in a moment.

Price's second suggestion is that, whereas dreams in this life are private experiences in which others have no life of their own (the only life they have is given to them by our dream), in our after-life we could expect real communication and interaction with other people with what, in this life, we call ESP. To follow this line of thinking, we can imagine that this communication and interaction could be of such a kind that our after-life could be experienced as if it were three dimensional, and could include touch, taste and smell. There could be many different worlds of people, each sharing the same telepathic community.

Thirdly, Price suggested that our after-life will be shaped not by the laws of physics but by the power of our desires –

the laws of psychology. Price imagined that our memories and desires would be carried with us to determine the images we experienced. So he cautions us against thinking that such an after-life would be an unqualified pleasant experience. The memories we take with us would reveal with unerring accuracy the real character of our desires – even those which are unpleasant or repressed. Should our memories and desires construct a hellish after-life for us, it could be that we would soon wish to modify our desires, so that eventually our desiring would bring us into what could be called the vision of God. Or, it could be, to follow John Hick, that our desiring becomes satisfied and we cease our desiring, so that our individual personal life fades and is absorbed into a supra-personal state of nirvana.

As interesting and plausible as this theory might at first appear, it has confounding difficulties. One objection Hick brings against this idea of our desires shaping our after-life is that, without the constraint of some equivalent to what we now experience of so-called natural laws, our lives would cease to develop if we did not have to face the disciplines and hazards of our environment.[8] But this objection is only valid if we enter life after death in an imperfect state, and a good case can be made that this is not so.

A more important objection to Price's theory is that his after-life is a delusion. It is questionable whether or not we could call his description of post-mortem existence *life* after death. From this present life we know that we are significantly shaped through interacting with others. But, in Price's proposed after-life there are, for us, no other people involved; they are only part of our memories, and "actors" in this dream-like world. Thus, this view of an after-life is a series of isolated individuals, not a community of interacting people that we know to be important to life. So, to follow Hick again, if we are going to have a truly interactive after-life we would have to give up the idea that each person's desires are sovereign. Instead, our after-life would be entering a world which was shaped by everyone's memories and desires.

While this view of our after-life may match an Old Testament theme of the eventual corporate unity of (at least God's) people, the individual is so lost in Price's theory that it should be abandoned as a reasonable description of what we could hope for beyond death. Also, from a traditional Christian perspective, an after-life that depends for its quality on the way we live this life and not on the intervention of God's transforming love has to be abandoned. For, as we will see, a central theme of biblical thought on life after death is that with God's intervention, we can experience the after-life as "heaven".

Despite initial expectations, Price's theory does not help us understand how we might live after death without a body. Nor, it turns out, does it help us resolve the problem as to whether or not we have a soul independent of our bodies.

## An astral body?

There is another suggested alternative for what we might experience in life after death without a body: having an astral body. According to this view, inside and shadowing what we usually think of as a person is another being of the same form, which is the real person. While our soul may not be thought to have any particular shape or be able to be measured, our so-called astral body can be imagined in this way, though it is to be thought of as more shadowy and ethereal in nature than our physical body.

Those who want to encourage us to think about our after-life along this line say that the best way to understand the astral body is to think of cinematic representations such as in the movie version of Noel Coward's *Blithe Spirit*. There a shadow person – visible only to some and only some of the time – detaches itself from a dead person and continues to live and participate in life. There may be some support for this view in Tertullian's writing. In his *De Anima* he describes the soul as having a bodily shape in the form of a human being in every respect (chapter 9). But we have to leave aside this view for it is no more than a variation of the view with which we have been dealing.

Indeed, as convincing as the argument is that we have a soul, we have not been able to develop a view of life after death that does not involve our body. At this point we will turn to the Bible to see how it can help in our thinking. Once again, our thinking is caught off balance by the biblical writers.

## The soul in the Bible

When we turn to the Bible, we are faced with ideas and thought patterns that are much more subtle and nuanced than some of the modern descriptions of our inner life which we have so far encountered.

In the Old Testament the word "soul" (*nephesh* in Hebrew) is used to describe that which makes us a living being. Thus at death a person breathes or pours out his or her "soul" (Genesis 35:18; Lamentations 2:12). The soul can be the seat of emotions such as love and joy, and is also associated with our will and moral actions.[9] The soul can even sum up the whole personality (1 Samuel 18:1) so that people are called souls (Exodus 1:5; Deuteronomy 10:22). The classic statement of the "soul" representing our whole person is Genesis 2:7: "The Lord . . . breathed into his nostrils the breath of life and the man became a living soul." That the "soul" is the whole person in the Old Testament can be seen when the word is used even for a recently dead person.[10]

Recalling what we said in chapter 2, for Old Testament writers the soul had no independent existence apart from the person who possesses or, more accurately, is it. The whole person is involved in the after-life, not just a person's "soul".

Indeed, Old Testament writers do not divide us into soul and body or into mind, soul and body; people are whole, integrated beings. This unity is not expressed by using the opposing concepts of body and soul, as did the Greeks and as we moderns tend to do, but by using the complementary and inseparable concepts of body and life.[11]

## The New Testament and the soul

Much of the thought patterns found in the Old Testament are reflected in the New Testament. The "soul" (*psuche* in Greek) can mean the place of emotion (Matthew 12:18; Luke 12:19), or the seat of life, or life itself.[12] The word "soul" can also be equivalent to "I", even for God, who would not be considered to have a soul separable from any other aspect of his person (Matthew 12:18; Hebrews 10:38).

Nevertheless, following a stream of tradition in the Old Testament, there is a hint in the New Testament that body and soul were thought to be at least distinct. In Matthew 10:28 Jesus is reported as saying that it was not necessary to fear the person who could only destroy the body; "rather fear the one who can destroy both soul and body in hell." We will be discussing this saying again in chapter seven. For the moment we can note that to take this statement to be full and sufficient support for life after death as involving only our independent soul is a mistake. Not only would this be a misunderstanding of Jesus' saying, it would also fail to take into account the importance of Jesus' resurrection in understanding the afterlife.

Paul gives us the clearest perspective of an early Christian writer's view of our inner life. In contrast to the Old Testament, Paul rarely uses the word soul. Most notably, he never uses the word for what survives after a person's death. This is because, as we will see, for Paul what life there is after death is a gift from God, not something inherently possible for humans. However, he reflects a Hebrew mind-set in using the word soul to designate the whole person (Romans 13:1) and sometimes a person's life (Romans 11:3; Philippians 2:30).

Particularly interesting is what Paul says in 1 Thessalonians 5:23. Some have tried to give an unnatural translation of the Greek so that it reads, "may your spirit, that is, your soul and body be kept sound." Also, the sentence has been divided to read, "May the God of peace sanctify you wholly and in every part. May both body and soul be preserved . . ." However, the most natural way to understand Paul is that he is saying, "may your spirit and soul and body be kept sound." In Hebrew and Greek both soul and spirit can refer to our breath or life force (Genesis 2:7; Job 27:3; Isaiah 57:16). However, prior to Paul there developed a distinction so that spirit referred more to our godward aspect and soul to the vital life force in us (1 Corinthians 2:13–15; 15:44–46). But, not only is this the only place in the New Testament where a person appears to be described as having three parts, it is also the first known three-part description of the human being. For this reason alone we should probably not be too quick to understand Paul (over against his Jewish heritage) dividing human life into three separate parts. Rather, Paul's prime concern in 1 Thessalonians 5:23 is probably to describe the whole person (compare Deuteronomy 6:5; Mark 12:30) as one who is not only to be understood to have a bodily and mental capacity but also open to appreciate the spiritual.

Another point at which we can catch a glimpse of a New Testament writer's understanding of our inner life is in Hebrews 4:12. The word of God is said to pierce "until it divides soul from spirit, joints from marrow." On a first reading this seems to be assuming that we have both a soul and a spirit. However, the writer is making the point that the word of God is doing something that is otherwise impossible, namely distinguishing between the indivisible soul and spirit. If this interpretation is correct, Hebrews 4:12 does not see our inner life composed of a soul and a spirit; they are indivisible.

## Conclusions

Do we have an immortal soul? Our answer to the question must be both "yes" and "no". Yes, we do have a soul. But our soul is not some independent spark of life or light that has been added to our inner life from outside by, say, God. Rather, from the very earliest days of our life, no less than our mind and body, our soul is an integral part of who we are and become.

We also have to say "no" in answer to our question. For from our discussion we can conclude that we cannot think of ourselves as having an immortal soul in the sense that after we die only our soul continues to live on without our body and mind. Our soul has no more independent existence than does our mind or body have an independent existence. Each of us is an integrated person. We see this not only from various sides of the debate. We also see it from the Bible.

From what we have seen from the Bible, there is no doubt that the writers consider that we have an inner life distinct from our body. But there is no evidence either that our inner life (our soul) or our outer life (our body) can exist separately. To the contrary, we are viewed as having inseparable parts or aspects. This leads us to an important conclusion: the widely-accepted idea among Christians and others (inherited from Greek philosophy) that we live on through the immortality of our souls (without our bodies) has to be called one of the greatest misunderstandings of Christianity.[13] This is confirmed when we take into account the famous passage in 1 Corinthians 15 about the resurrection of the dead. This is to anticipate the next chapter.

## Notes

[1] Plato, *Phaedrus* 245c6–246a2, 245e; *Timaeus* 35a–b; 42d6–e1–4.

[2] See Plato, *Phaedo* 70d7–72e2; 72e3–77d5; 78b4–80e1; *Republic* 608d3–611a2.

[3] Richard Swinburne, *The Evolution of the Soul* (Oxford: Clarendon, 1997), pp. 145–60, 322–32.

[4] Søren Kierkegaard, *The Concept of Anxiety* (Princeton, NJ: Princeton University Press, 1980), p. 43.

[5] Compare John Macquarie, *In Search of Humanity* (London: SCM, 1982), chapter 5.

[6] An obvious point brought to my attention in private communication by Brenton Wait.

[7] Compare Keith Ward, *The Battle for the Soul* (London: Hodder & Stoughton, 1985), chapter 7.

[8] So John Hick, *Death and Eternal Life* (Louisville, KY: Westminster/John Knox, 1994), p. 273.

[9] See Psalm 86:4; Song of Solomon 1:7; cf. Job 7:15; Psalms 25:1; 119:167.

[10] Leviticus 19:28; 22:4; Numbers 5:2; 9:6, 10; Haggai 2:13

[11] So Edmond Jacob, "*psuche*" in Gerhard Kittel, et al., ed., *Theological Dictionary of the New Testament*, vol. 9 (Grand Rapids: Eerdmans, 1974), pp. 620–21, 631.

[12] See Matthew 6:25; Mark 8:35; 10:45.

[13] So also Oscar Cullmann, *Immortality of the Soul or Resurrection of the Dead? Witness of the New Testament* (London: Epworth, 1958), p. 15.

# 5

## Will We Have Bodies?

For some readers we will have already come to the startling conclusion that one of the greatest misunderstandings of Christianity is the idea that we live on through the immortality of our souls. The biblical perspective is – in line with many modern ways of thinking – that we are so thoroughly both body and soul that our after-life has to involve our body: our resurrection! But what kind of body will we have? And when will we receive this body? Will it be when we die or will we all be resurrected at the end of time? Answering these questions with their various complications is the task of this chapter.

# Will We Have Bodies?

"We will all be changed, in a moment,
in the twinkling of an eye . . . the dead will be
raised imperishable . . . for this imperishable body
must put on imperishability"
Paul of Tarsus

"My soul is not I, and if only souls are saved,
I am not saved, nor is any man"
Thomas Aquinas

We have had to set aside a number of possibilities in thinking clearly about life after death. In the first chapter we set aside the most fundamental option, that there is no life after death. We saw that from a number of different perspectives it is reasonable to believe that there is life after death. We have also had to set aside the idea that life after death involves any form of reincarnation. The most common belief – even among Christians – that only our soul (or our mind or personality) lives on after death has also had to be put aside. We saw that not only is the idea of the immortality of the soul inconsistent with traditional Christianity: it is also incompatible with our understanding of what constitutes a person. If only our soul lives on, it would not be us that would be living after death, only a part of us.

To be a person in the after-life requires our body, at least in some form. Therefore, in this chapter we will consider the idea of our resurrection. This is expressed in its simplest form in the epitaph Benjamin Franklin wrote for himself:

The body of B. Franklin, Printer, Like the Cover of an old Book, Its Contents torn out, And stript of its Lettering and Gilding, Lies here, Food for Worms. But the work shall not be lost; for it will, as he believ'd, appear once more in a new and more elegant Edition Corrected and improved By the Author.

At this point many people – including important philosophers of our present as well as earlier times – will want to part company with us when we entertain any idea of our resurrection. The problems encountered in the concept are thought to be very great.

First, if our resurrection takes place immediately after we die, it obviously does not involve the body we used on earth for it has never been reported (except in the case of Jesus of Nazareth!) that, soon or immediately after death, a person's body unaccountably disappeared, presumably for use in the after-life. Therefore, if we are going to think clearly about our life after death we will have to dismiss the idea that, immediately we die, our after-life involves the body we were using on earth.

Secondly, if our resurrection is to take place some time in the future, perhaps hundreds or even millions of years after we die, there is a similar problem. Archaeologists are continually unearthing the bodily remains of dead people. Presumably some of them would have been eligible for a positive life after death. But if their resurrection is still to take place in the future, their complete bodies no longer exist. Most of the atoms that constituted their bodies are no longer available for their supposed resurrection. They have been changed into other forms of energy. Indeed, if we allow our line of thought some freedom, we can imagine an ongoing cycle in which some of the atoms from dead people have made their way into the nutrients of plants, which have made their way into animals, which have made their way into the food of later human beings. This means that at some future resurrection there will be some atoms that have been a part of perhaps quite a number of people. As bizarre as this line of thought may be, it illustrates the great difficulty we have in maintaining that the body we are using on earth will be directly involved in our after-life in any way similar to the way it is involved in our earthly life. Of course, we could take the view that a God who performs miracles could accomplish such a feat. But I am not sure God could perform such a miracle, any more than he can change the past or make square circles.

Therefore, after noting the centrality of this belief in traditional Christianity, in this chapter we will be exploring the idea that our after-life involves our resurrection. We will do this, first, through examining what the New Testament writers (notably Paul) have to say. Then, secondly, we will see how the early church fathers developed the idea, as well as the problems they encountered. However, thirdly, because the traditional description of our resurrection is now seen to be thoroughly impractical we will need to take another step in looking at contemporary options which involve some form of body. Finally, I will attempt to set out a view of life after death that is both consistent with New Testament ideas about life after death and which we can more readily take up.

## The New Testament: Paul

As opposed to reincarnation (see chapter 3) and immortality (see chapter 4), it was the doctrine of resurrection which, from the beginning, became an important part of traditional Christianity. While other New Testament writers mention the resurrection of the dead,[1] it is Paul who is the chief biblical exponent of the idea that our after-life will revolve around our bodies being resurrected. Therefore we will focus our attention on examining key passages from his letters.

## Resurrection? 1 Corinthians 15

In 1 Corinthians 15 Paul deals at length with the problem of our resurrection. Not surprisingly Paul's readers appear to object to the resurrection of the dead on the grounds that it is unimaginable. He is probably citing his readers when he says: "How are the dead raised? With what kind of body are they provided?" (1 Corinthians 15:35, my translation). This provides the impetus for Paul's discussion of the resurrection of the dead.

He begins by setting out what had been handed on to him about the resurrection of Jesus (1 Corinthians 15:1–11). He then moves on to debate with those who denied the resurrection of the dead (15:12–34). From his discussion we can detect four grounds for his believing in the resurrection of the dead.

First, there is what seems to be a circular argument starting at an unexpected point. He does not start where we might expect with the resurrection of Christ as the ground for resurrection. He does not even start with the general idea of the resurrection of the dead, as a first reading of verse 12 could suggest. Rather, the basis of his argument for our resurrection is verse 14: "if Christ has not been raised, then our proclamation has been in vain and your faith has been in vain." Paul's starting point for his argument is the experience of the Corinthians in response to his proclamation. From what we see in other places, in this letter, this experience would have been one of "demonstration of the Spirit and of power . . . of God" (1 Corinthians 2:4; see also 4:20). Therefore, their belief in the resurrection of Christ and the resurrection of the dead is thought to be based on their having already experienced God's power raising them to life in this life.

From this starting point, secondly, the main part of his argument is that since Jesus has risen from the dead it follows that there is a resurrection of the dead, for he is the first fruit of those who have died (1 Corinthians 15:20; also Acts 26:23; Hebrews 6:20).

Thirdly, another point he offers for believing in the resurrection of the dead is that, "If the dead are not raised at all, why are people baptized on their behalf?" (1 Corinthians 15:29). On a first reading it seems that Paul's readers are being baptized on behalf of unbelieving friends who have died. From what we know about Paul's thinking (that people gain a relationship with God or obtain life after death not through any ceremony but only through putting their trust in him), it is puzzling that he should refer to the practice of proxy baptism without showing disapproval (see Galatians 3:1–6; also Ephesians 2:8–9). Therefore, it could be that Paul is referring to Christians among his readers who are being baptized so they can be reunited with their departed Christian friends. Whatever interpretation we adopt, Paul's point is that if those who are reading his letter do not believe in the resurrection of the dead, why do they practise a baptism of proxy that involves the dead?

Fourthly, Paul also argues for the resurrection of the dead on the grounds that he would not put himself in mortal danger every hour if there was not the hope of resurrection (1 Corinthians 15:30–34).

If we are to believe that our bodies are going to be resurrected for the after-life, we still have the problem of understanding what kind of body will be involved.

## What kind of body?

From verse 35 Paul turns to answer his readers' questions about the kind of body they can expect to have in the after-life. We may not be convinced by every point of his argument. But here it is: first he argues that our earthly body will die and be replaced by a resurrected body in the same way that a seed planted in the ground dies and is replaced by a plant (1 Corinthians 15:36–38). We might object to this argument by saying that this implies that our resurrected body will be a part of (or at least making direct use of) our earthly body, for a plant is of the same material as the seed. However, this is not what Paul has in mind. He understands that the seed dies (15:36) and that God provides the new body of the plant (15:38). That is, in Paul's view, our resurrected body is connected to and continuous with but different from our earthly body. Behind this argument was the well-known principle that life comes through death (compare Mark 8:35; John 12:24).

Secondly, Paul says that just as there are different kinds of flesh (human, animal, bird and fish) so there are both earthly and heavenly bodies (1 Corinthians 15:39–41). He adds to this argument that just as there are different "glories" – one for the sun, another for the moon, and another for the stars – so there is a difference between the earthly and heavenly body.

Paul concludes from these two points that resurrection means *transformation*. There is something very important about this transformation which we need to note. In his use of the word "flesh" (*sarx*, 1 Corinthians 15:39, 44, 50) we can see that Paul considers that our transformation will not be the relegation of our earthly or fleshly body but will involve a change from our earthly body into our heavenly body (1 Corinthians 15:40).

Thirdly, in the light of establishing a variety among the types of bodies (human, animal, bird and fish), Paul then moves on to say something more specific about the resurrected body; he says that it will be a spiritual body with the glory of God (1 Corinthians 15:43–44). We will come across this same point when we examine Philippians 3:21. To help his readers understand this idea, he says that the first man (Adam) was from earth and the second man (Jesus) is from heaven (1 Corinthians 15:47). From this he concludes that, "Just as we have borne the image of the man of dust, we will also bear the image of the man of heaven" (15:49). In other words, just as

God created a life-body for the first Adam, so God will create a spirit-body for us, as he has already done in Jesus.

Paul supports his case by saying that this change from our earthly bodies to a heavenly body is essential. It is essential, for neither the living ("flesh and blood") nor the dead ("perishable") can inherit the (spiritual and immortal) kingdom of God (1 Corinthians 15:50). That means, Paul concludes, that not only the living but also the dead will need to be changed or transformed in a moment, in the twinkling of an eye (15:51–52) so that, at least in the case of those who are alive when this event takes place, people can be expected to take on imperishable and immortal bodies. Paul is making the point that the living as much as the dead and decaying need to be transformed. In passing, we can note that Paul assumes that this transformation is to take place at "the End"; "at the last trumpet" (compare Joel 2:1; Zephaniah 1:16), when he himself will still be alive (1 Corinthians 15:51).

Drawing together what we have discovered from 1 Corinthians 15 about Paul's understanding of the nature of our resurrected body, the following points stand out. First, as a seed is discontinuous with but related to the plant so will our resurrected bodies be related to but discontinuous with our earthly bodies. In expressing this mysterious continuity (it will still be us) yet different (we will no longer be subject to the power of death), Paul has used a number of contrasts to help his readers grasp his thinking about the nature of our resurrection body:

| | | |
|---|---|---|
| Perishable | – | Imperishable |
| Mortal | – | Immortal |
| Dishonourable | – | Glorious |
| Weak | – | Powerful |
| Physical | – | Spiritual |

Secondly, this new life is not simply life after death; this is life beyond the realm and power of death. For when our bodies are made immortal, death will have no impact on us (1 Corinthians 15:54–55). Also, for Paul, our imperishability, immortality, glory, power and also the spiritual nature of our resurrected body is not something inherent in us. The verb (in the middle voice) "put on" is a clear signal that our imperishability is a gift supplied by God. With this gift of a new body we clothe ourselves (15:53–54). God's work is not even a restoration of something that has been damaged in human beings. The resurrected body is a new action of creation by God.

Thirdly, in traditional Christianity the resurrection of Jesus is taken to be the cornerstone of the belief that there is such a thing as the resurrection of the dead for others. We have seen that such an intrinsic link is no less important to Paul (compare 1 Corinthians 15:12). But we have seen that the starting point of his argument for resurrection is our experience in this life (1 Corinthians 15:14).

Reading between the lines of 1 Corinthians 15:12 it seems that Paul is replying to those who accept his proclamation that Christ rose from the dead, but who do not accept that others will be involved in a resurrection after their death. He points out the absurdity of such a position, for the one is linked to the other. He goes on to say that the resurrection of Christ and the resurrection of the dead, as well as their faith, are all of a piece, so that if Christ has not been raised not only is *their* faith in vain but also *he* will have been found to be a false witness to God.

### Resurrection? Philippians

Philippians 3:21a says that when Christ returns from heaven, "He will transform the body of our humiliation that it may be conformed to the body of his glory." As we have seen a number of times, "the body" for Paul is not a container for the person. The body is the person, even though that body and person are frail and subject to death. However, Paul says here that when Christ returns he will, by his power (3:21b), transform our bodies to make them like his body of glory, that is, his spiritual body (compare 1 Corinthians 15:43–44). This life after death is more strictly life beyond death, for Paul is assuming Christ's return will take place in his lifetime and will not involve the body being separated from the other aspects of life. Rather, like Christ whose resurrection determines the nature of our life beyond the grave, our resurrection will involve being transformed into a spiritual body. It is also not that our resurrected body will consist in being a spirit. Instead, keeping in mind the contrasts between the earthly and resurrection body we listed above, our new body will be so determined and motivated by the Spirit that it will exist in a way that enables our bodies – us – to live completely in the spiritual realm.

### The New Testament: 1 Peter

Apart from Paul, the first letter of Peter also says something about the nature of the resurrected Jesus, the general resurrection and the relationship between the two.

In two parallel phrases 1 Peter says that Christ "was put to death in the flesh, but made alive in the spirit" (1 Peter 3:18). This is an unmistakable reference to Jesus' death and resurrection. On a first reading this could be taken to mean that Jesus died bodily but came alive as a spirit. A closer reading leads us to a different conclusion.

In the New Testament "flesh" and "spirit" normally refer to two modes of existence or ways of living. Flesh represents human nature and the life we live without any particular reference to God. Spirit represents the life we live in the light of God entering human affairs. Before we can use this information to understand what 1 Peter is saying we need, also, to have in mind two creed-like statements in the New Testament.

In Romans 1:3–4 Paul says that Jesus "was descended from David according to the flesh and was declared to be Son of God with power according to the spirit". And 1 Timothy 3:16 says that "He was revealed in the flesh, vindicated in spirit."

With these statements in mind, we can see that for 1 Peter to say that Jesus was "made alive in the spirit" was probably meant to convey the idea that his still bodily existence was now in the sphere in which God's Spirit was powerfully at work. Jesus was now without human limitation (see 1 Peter 1:21) for he had been made alive by the Spirit (see Romans 8:11). Therefore, it is not the case that Jesus' body died and his immortal soul was raised. That is a later Greek understanding of the passage.[2] Rather, Jesus' body had been raised into God's spiritual realm.

A little later, 1 Peter says something about the nature of life after death for the believer: "the gospel was proclaimed even to the dead, so that, though they had been judged in the flesh as everyone is judged, they might live in the spirit as God does" (1 Peter 4:6). This cryptic sentence is alluding to well-known ideas of the time that, even though God's people suffer and appear to be condemned by their fellow human beings, God will vindicate them.[3]

There is no reason to identify the dead mentioned in 1 Peter here with the spirits to which Christ made a proclamation in Hades (1 Peter 3:19). Rather, as the remainder of this verse (4:6) implies, the dead are those (Christians) who had heard and responded to the gospel before they died and are now, therefore, living "in the spirit as God does." This last phrase "as God does" is part of a balanced pair with "in the flesh" used earlier in the verse. Thus 1 Peter means that the dead – like Christ of 3:18 – are living in God's realm, or before God.

The life after death that 1 Peter is describing could be referring to a future resurrection of the dead. But, as he has already been referring to the contrast between Christ's human life and present life "in the spirit" (1 Peter 3:18), 1 Peter is again telling us that life after death involves being raised into God's spiritual realm.

## The resurrected body of Jesus

Behind the texts we have been examining is the assumption that Jesus' resurrection body was continuous with the one that existed before he was crucified. Thus it is the view of the gospel writers that Jesus appeared after his death in a way that made him recognizable as the same person he was before he was crucified (Luke 24:30–31; John 20:15–18). He could eat fish (Luke 24:43), and his body could be touched (John 20:27). Yet the gospel writers also assign profoundly different characteristics to the risen body of Jesus. His body was no longer subject to some of the limitations we presently experience. He could pass through a locked door (John 20:19, 26); he could suddenly materialize – at first unrecognized – next to two of his followers (Luke 24:15–16); and he was able to vanish on the Mount of Olives (Acts 1:9). It is this not-too-carefully-described body, released from some of its human limitations, which we can expect to be the model for our bodies in the after-life.

## When?

When will we receive our resurrected body? With Jesus the answer is known and straightforward. He died and three days later his earthly body was transformed into his risen body. A problem arises when we inquire about the time of our own resurrection and transformation.

Some people have found in the Bible the idea that we will be resurrected at the moment of our death; others have pointed to texts to argue that it will be at "the End" when we will be resurrected. Still others see evidence that, at death, we will have to wait until "the End" to receive our resurrected body.

Part of the reason for these different views is that not only have texts been forced by various schools of thought to conform to their beliefs, but that different New Testament writers seem to express different views. However, in that Paul appears to express all three positions we can expect to be able to resolve the problem relatively easily if we can understand his thinking behind his apparent contradictions. First we will look at each of the three views expressed by Paul.

## 1. At our death

In Philippians 1:23 it seems that our resurrection will take place at our own death. Paul says that he has the "desire to depart and be with Christ". In this statement, death means being immediately with Christ. Keeping in mind what he says in 1 Corinthians 15:50–52 (about being transformed in the twinkling of an eye, see above) this means Paul would expect to be resurrected or transformed at his death.

Paul's view is supported by two passages in Luke. First is the story Jesus told of a rich man and a poor man named Lazarus. The poor man dies and is "carried away by the angels to be with Abraham" (Luke 16:22). Even if this death is intended to be like the immediate translation to heaven without death experienced by Enoch (Genesis 5:24) and Elijah (2 Kings 2:11), Lazarus is still immediately experiencing the full and intimate divine care in his life after death (compare *Testament of Abraham* 20A).

The second passage, expressing a similar view to Paul, is Luke 23:43. Jesus says to the repentant thief on the cross next to him, "today you will be with me in paradise." There is no doubt about where Jesus and the thief will be after death, for "paradise" was a symbol for heaven (see 2 Corinthians 12:4; Revelation 2:7). And paradise is going to be experienced at death "today" (see Luke 5:26). There have been unsuccessful attempts at a rather forced interpretation that takes "today" not as the calendar day of the crucifixion but more generally as the "day" or "today of salvation" (see Luke 2:11; 4:21). This would mean that our resurrection is understood to take place not on the day of our death but on "the Day" or at "the End". The advantage of this interpretation is that it brings this text into line with those texts (see below) which seem to imply that our resurrection will take place at "the End", or at least at a time later than our death. But it is a forced interpretation of the text which – if applied more widely to include our expected experience – most naturally reads as a promise of being in paradise when we die (Acts 7:54–60).

## 2. We will experience a waiting period

On a first reading, both Paul and the writer of the book of Revelation seem to hold the view that there will be a waiting period between our death and receiving our resurrected body. In 1 Thessalonians 4:13–18 Paul writes that he does not want his readers to be uninformed about those who have "fallen asleep". He believes that when Christ descends from heaven he will bring with him those who have fallen asleep, through calling them to rise first. Then those who are alive, who are left, will be caught up in the clouds together with them (compare 2 Corinthians 4:14) to meet the Lord in the air, so that we will all be with the Lord for ever.

Paul is often understood to be assuming that there is a waiting period between our death and our resurrection when he says that those who have died are asleep. But this is an incorrect interpretation, for in antiquity "sleep" was simply a polite way of talking about death (1 Kings 2:10; Daniel 12:2). Therefore we cannot conclude from Paul saying the dead are asleep, that he thought that after we die we remain asleep – waiting – until we are resurrected at "the End".

Indeed, one of the key points of 2 Corinthians 5:3 is that there will be no waiting period between our death and our resurrection. Paul says when we die "we will not be found naked". Perhaps with the constant threat of death (see

2 Corinthians 1:8–10; 4:10–12), Paul considers that he may die before "the End". However, since writing 1 Corinthians, Paul has not changed his mind about the nature of the resurrected body: made by God, it will replace our earthly body destroyed at death (2 Corinthians 5:1). But so instantaneous is this transformation (1 Corinthians 15:52) – there will be no time of nakedness or waiting (2 Corinthians 5:3) – that he goes on to use the idea of the new body being like a coat put over our earthly body.

Revelation 6:9 and 11 is another place where a writer seems to suggest there will be a waiting period between our death and our resurrection. The writer says that when the Lamb opened the fifth seal he saw under the altar the souls of those who had been slaughtered for the word of God. They are given a white robe and told to wait. However, these souls are not incomplete partial people waiting to be made whole. In the book of Revelation the word "soul" is used not of a constituent inner part of life but for the whole of a human life (Revelation 12:11; 18:13). Also, the "souls" are not being described as incomplete people, for they are given white robes to wear. Further, that they are said to be under the altar means that they are already in the presence of the one who sat on it (see Babylonian Talmud *Shabbath* 152b). Importantly, the waiting is not for something they do not have, but for others to join them.

Therefore, the idea that there is a waiting period for the dead between our death and our resurrection at "the End" arises from a misunderstanding of Paul's use of "sleep" and also from Revelation's use of "waiting". From what we learn from Paul and the writer of Revelation, we can expect our bodies to be immediately transformed at the point of death. The waiting is not for anything we will not have at the point of death but for others to join us.

## 3. The End

The interpretation we have given of sleeping and waiting may resolve the tension between the ideas of the instantaneous reception of our resurrected bodies and our having to wait. However, we still have to understand how Paul can say our individual resurrection or transformation takes place not at our individual death but at "the End". In 1 Corinthians 15:51–52 Paul says that those who have already died, along with those remaining alive, will all be changed at "the last trumpet". (This was a Jewish idea for "the End", which Paul also used in 1 Thessalonians 4:16.[4])

## The resolution?

When do we receive our resurrected body: the moment we die (Philippians 1:23), after a period of waiting (1 Thessalonians 4:13-18), or at "the End" (1 Corinthians 15:51–52)? If Paul expects no interval of time between our death and receiving the resurrected body (2 Corinthians 5:3; Philippians 1:23), yet some will have died before the second coming when the resurrection is to take place (1 Corinthians 15:52) for everyone (2 Corinthians 4:14; 1 Thessalonians 4:17), a reasonable explanation is this: Paul thought that in the consciousness of those who had died there was no interval of waiting between their death and the second coming. Only for those (like us!) remaining alive before "the End" does there appear to be a period of waiting for those who have already died. It is in this interpretation that we find the reason why so little is said about the interim period between death and resurrection – it only exists for those of us still alive.

## The early church fathers

When we see what was believed about our resurrected body in the first few centuries after the New Testament times, we begin to see the superiority of Paul's view. The church fathers had a fundamentally different belief about the nature of the resurrection of the body. While Paul rarely used the word "flesh" in his discussion of our future life (he generally talked of the resurrection of our "body"), the early fathers focused on the idea that it would be a resurrection of our "flesh". In this way they were able to emphasize the reality of the resurrection body and its continuity with our present body. This is what is behind Saint Augustine saying that, "every soul will have its own body" (*Enchiridion* 87). Much later, John Donne's sonnets expressed this same view:

> At the round earths imagin'd corners, blow
> your trumpets, Angells, and arise, arise
> From death, you numberlesse infinities
> Of soules, and to your scattred bodies goe.[5]

A Latin scholar Tyrannius Rufinus (AD 345–410) said that "particles composing each individual's flesh" would have to be collected together for our resurrection (*Apostles' Creed* §42). Even more graphic was Augustine. He said that in the resurrection the cannibal would restore the flesh he had borrowed (*City of God* 22:20).

In the beginning of this chapter I pointed out some of the bizarre and amusing problems that arise from the idea that the material particles of our bodies will be reassembled for our after-life. Nevertheless, the early fathers were committed to the resurrection of our "flesh", for a number of good reasons.

First, the early fathers were right to say our life could not be conceived without a body. Justin Martyr considered that for God to save human beings by saving only their souls without raising their bodies would not be to save the whole person. He put it clearly: "Is the soul by itself man? No; but the soul of man. Would the body be called man? No, but it is called the body of man. If, then, neither of these is by itself man, but that which is made up of the two together is called man, and God has called *man* to life and resurrection, he has called not a part, but the whole, which is the soul and the body."[6] This view, which continues to reflect even much of our contemporary thinking about the resurrection of the body, is summed up in the frequently quoted saying of Thomas Aquinas: "My soul is not I, and if only souls are saved, I am not saved, nor is any man."

Secondly, Justin Martyr argued that the resurrection of the body is assured, because God would not neglect our bodies any more than a builder would neglect a house he had built. Others, including Athenagoras, for example, the second century Christian apologist from Athens, argued similarly for the resurrection of the body, adding that the creation of human beings would have been pointless if there was to be no afterlife.[7]

Thirdly, the fathers considered they had good biblical support for the view that our flesh would be resurrected.[8] They pointed to a number of passages, especially to the story of the valley of dry bones in Ezekiel 37, where God is said to reassemble the bones and bodies of the dead.[9] However, this story is not written out of a belief that dead people's bodies will be reconstituted; it is a vision of God bringing life to his defeated and discouraged people.

Also, as we saw in chapter 2, so far as modern scholarship finds support for a fleshly or bodily resurrection in the Old Testament, it is generally seen to be restricted to Isaiah 26:19 and Daniel 12:2. In the New Testament, Romans 8:11 might be seen as supporting the fathers' teaching that there would be a fleshly resurrection.[10] There Paul says that Christ "will give life to your mortal bodies". But a careful reading of the verse shows it cannot be used in this way. In the context of verse 10 the mortal body is not simply the fleshly body but our embodiment in this world, expressed in our mortality and corruptibility. Indeed, the early fathers had great difficulty contending with such statements as "flesh and blood cannot inherit the kingdom of God" (1 Corinthians 15:50).

Fourthly, the most important argument for the resurrection of our flesh – offered by almost all the early church fathers – was that Jesus rose from the dead in the flesh and was the first fruits of our resurrection. Once again, what the early fathers are defending – Jesus' resurrection being our model – is to be applauded. However, from our discussion of Paul's thinking we can see that he was thinking of the spiritual transformation of our body rather than of a simple resuscitation of our present physical bodies.

In proposing such views, it is not that the early church fathers were simply part of an unscientific and incredulous society. For example, Augustine found himself having to make a case that, despite their natural weight, human bodies could live in the sky. He knew the difficulty of what he was proposing, because he argued that just as humans can make boats that are heavier than water float on water, surely God could do the same with our bodies. He pointed out that surely God, who can create birds to fly, could do the same for human beings so they can be in heaven. And he says that, if the earth can hang without support, then there is no reason to doubt that a human body could stay up in heaven (*City of God* 13:18; 22:11).

Nevertheless, what is important about these strange views from the early church fathers is that they show us their commitment to the idea that we are not to expect our life after death to be only our souls living on. Also, by way of contrast, their fantastic views reinforce the merit of taking our cue from Paul in maintaining that in our after-life our body will have been transformed so that we can live in the spiritual realm.

## Traditional Christianity

For many years the doctrine of the resurrection of our *fleshly* body was assured a place in traditional Christianity through the work of Thomas Aquinas.[11] Even though the French Protestant reformer John Calvin saw the practical difficulties, he took the resurrection of Christ and the power of God to be the assurance our faith needed to overcome any obstacles.[12] Martin Luther (1483–1546) also supported the idea that we can expect our fleshly body to be resurrected in our after-life (*Larger Catechism* 2:60). The fourth of the *Thirty-nine Articles* of the Church of England also affirms the resurrection of Christ and its nature, in saying that he "took again his body, with flesh, bones, and all things appertaining to the perfection of Man's nature". And, in *The Book of Common Prayer* (1662), there is a provision for anointing the sick. The minister asks the sick person to affirm that they believe in the resurrection of the flesh.

However, most people now find the idea to be ridiculous and impossible that our fleshly body will one day (possibly in the distant future) be reassembled and reanimated. It is reasonable to ask, for example, how a body that has been buried at sea for 1,000 years is to be resurrected; or how a body is to be brought back together which, many centuries ago, was eaten by a cannibal who was subsequently eaten by another cannibal. And, how is it comprehensible that the vapours and long-decomposed, charred remains of a saint burnt at the stake in the Middle Ages will be reassembled to live again with the same fleshly body he or she had in this life?

Augustine suggested that our resurrected fleshly body – modelled on Christ's resurrected body – could be called spiritual and could take part in the glory of God because the flesh was now subservient to the spirit.[13]

## Five contemporary alternatives

Despite Augustine's argument, the idea that our present bodies will be reconstituted and revived is both too simplistic (at least for what Paul had in mind) and, in fact, in conflict with what he had in mind. It is also incomprehensible, if not amusing, to most people who are trying to think clearly about life after death.

Attempting to do justice to both biblical and church tradition, as well as trying to avoid some of the absurd implications of thinking that we will be involved in a *fleshly* resurrection, a number of alternative ways of understanding our afterlife have been suggested. We have already had to set aside the view that our life after death will involve the immortality of our soul, not only because it is one of the greatest misunderstandings of Christianity, but also because it runs counter to what we now see constitutes our real existence.

On the one hand we understand that our real existence involves both our non-physical or inner self (sometimes called our soul or mind or personality), as well as our physical body. On the other hand the Bible teaches that the whole person, including the body, is involved in the after-life. But how? It is tempting to say no more than that all attempts to describe our future life are inadequate. But this is not helpful. What then are our alternatives?

## 1. Our exact replication

John Hick has suggested that we think of our resurrected life as the divine creation of an exact mind-and-body replica of ourselves in another space (heaven). Before we reject this view out of hand as incomprehensible, we need to take into account the idea of Norbert Wiener (1894–1964), the American mathematician. His idea was that our bodies are not a static form (like a stone) but rather a pattern of change (like a flame). This means that, at least in principle, we can view our bodies as a message that can be coded, transmitted and then decoded or translated back into its original form, just as sound can be changed into radio waves, transmitted to a different place and translated back into sound.[14]

Because of our experience of dreaming, in which our memory is used in both our real and dream world, we can imagine the possibility of living in a different dimension or space. However, the idea of our resurrected life being through our replication has too many problems to be useful. For example, we would have to take on the sad view that the maimed would be resurrected as such, rather than enjoy the use of a complete body. As Hick himself acknowledges, an exact replica of a dying person would be a dying person in the last moments of life, which means that the first thing the person would do in the resurrected life would be to die! Even if we suppose that the replicated, resurrected person was the person at the peak of his or her life, the person would be resurrected without the memories and character development of later life.

## 2. We will be temporarily disembodied

According to this theory, after death we will exist in an incomplete state as immaterial souls. Later, at "the End" of time, God will miraculously raise up our bodies from the ground, transforming them into glorified bodies and reuniting them with our souls, making us complete again.[15]

Support for the view that we can exist (at least temporarily) apart from our bodies is sought from Paul. He says in 2 Corinthians 5:6 that "while we are at home in the body we are away from the Lord." From this it is deduced that Paul thinks it is possible for us to live without our bodies. But it is a forced understanding of what Paul has in mind. From what we have seen already, we know that Paul understands the whole person to be involved in the resurrection. And here he is not assuming two parts of a person but distinguishing between his or her earthly and heavenly body. That is, what Paul is saying here is that, "to be at home in [this] body" is to be away from the Lord.

In the same letter, Paul talks about being caught up to the third heaven, "whether in the body or out of the body I did not know" (2 Corinthians 12:2). On a first reading it looks as if Paul could consider it possible to exist without a body. However, in the context of his letter, Paul's intentions are entirely different. Earlier in the letter when he said that "we will not be found naked" (2 Corinthians 5:3), he is making it clear that we will not exist after death without a body. Further, Paul is writing to people who would probably have been aware of the Gnostic view that the body was evil and that authentic spiritual experiences took place outside the body (compare Philo, *On Dreams* 1:36). Thus it is highly unlikely that Paul would be proposing that we can exist without our bodies. Rather, in writing carefully in the face of a dilemma, he does not want to say he was in the body, for that may suggest that the experience was less than what it could be. But he also does not want to say that he was out of the body for that would deny that he was totally involved in the experience. Therefore, he says, "God only knows" (2 Corinthians 12:2).

Further, the idea that we will be temporarily disembodied after we die is thought to reconcile the view that the general resurrection will take place at "the End" with the view that at death we will immediately be in paradise (compare Luke 23:43). According to this view, the thief who died on a cross next to Jesus would be with Jesus in paradise on the day of his death, but he would be in the form of a disembodied spirit waiting to be bodily raised much later at "the End". However, we have already seen that the apparent conflict between being with Jesus at death, yet waiting to be raised on the Last Day, is easily explained if this is taken to be the perspective of those still living (see above). In short, the view that we will be temporarily disembodied is both unnecessary and – to repeat our conclusions from above – also based on a misunderstanding of Paul.

### 3. Our present bodies will be connected with our resurrected bodies

Another alternative to understanding the place of our body in our after-life is based on Paul's analogy of the dead seed growing into a plant (1 Corinthians 15:35–44). According to this view, our earthly body is like a seed being planted in the soil. What comes up is not the seed but a new plant. What rises in our resurrection is not our physical body but a new spiritual body which, in some way, has grown out of the physical one and adapted to the spiritual existence of life after death.[16] Such a direct relationship between our earthly body and our heavenly body is still difficult to comprehend when we think about how long-dead and dissipated and dispersed corpses are going to be able to be reassembled and used in such a way. Hence we need to look at other suggestions.

### 4. Our bodies will not be used in our resurrection bodies

This is now the most popular view. In a nutshell, this view is that for our resurrection our physical bodies will not be restored, even in a glorified form. There will be no physical or material continuity between our earthly body and the body we will have in the resurrected life. Instead, God will give us new bodies like the risen Lord's. For example, Alec Vidler (1899–1991), an Anglican priest and one-time dean of King's College, Cambridge, said that in eternity we will possess spiritual organisms equivalent to, but different from, the physical bodies we have now.[17] When we inquire what this spiritual body will be like, this view does not allow us to be very specific. Those who hold this view describe our resurrected body in terms such as our personality, or our personal identity, or the person we have become, or the full integrity of our humanity, or the vital principle of what we are, or the law of our constitution, or our formal identity, or the traces of our memory or disposition.[18]

This view is certainly much easier to comprehend than that proposed by the early church fathers. However, without in some way involving our present physical bodies in our resurrected life, it would be difficult to argue that we will be the same person we are here. And we have not done justice to what Paul had in mind. Therefore we turn to a further suggestion.

## 5. Our present bodies will be used in our resurrected bodies

For this concept, Jesus is taken as the model. That is, in describing our resurrection we can take our cue from the resurrection of Jesus, whose dead body was somehow transformed into a different mode of existence. Without remainder, his body was taken up into and superseded by his new way of existing, as fuel is used for energy. However, in view of the incomprehensibility of this happening for individuals whose bodies have been long decomposed, used and reused in other forms of life, there is an important modification.

Professor C. F. D. Moule (b. 1908) of Cambridge University has suggested that it is conceivable that the total matter of this time-space world will not be "scrapped" but used up (recycled!) by God to create another existence. This would not be creation out of nothing into nothing (*ex nihilo in nihilo*) but creation out of nothing into something new (*ex nihilo in aliquid novi*). Professor Moule suggests that perhaps all the material of humankind returns to the collective reservoir of the totality of matter which one day could be used by the Creator as the material for our new existence.[19]

An obvious assumption of this view is that our resurrection cannot be considered in terms of known physics, or a smooth transition from this life to our resurrected life. A significant miracle on the scale of creation is required.

The attractiveness of this view is that it takes seriously the resurrection of Jesus being the first fruits of the resurrection of believers. That is, Jesus can be seen to anticipate an ultimate plan of God for using up the material world, including our bodies, into what is transmaterial or spiritual. Also this view overcomes the bizarre idea that our scattered and decomposed bodies are separated from other matter and reassembled for our resurrection. In the light of all these views, what can we now believe if we are thinking clearly about our resurrection?

## A way forward?

Once again, as attractive and straightforward as it may be to think of our life after death in terms of the immortality of our soul (or mind or personality), it is an impoverished view that short-changes the beauty and depth of the Christian perspective on the after-life. In any case, no support can be found in the Bible for this view.

It is because of the longstanding influence of the bizarre ideas developed from the days of the early church fathers, that the biblical views (notably from Paul) have been overshadowed. This has caused an unnecessary struggle to hold together the idea of a resurrection with what we understand about the nature of a person as involving both the inner (non-material) and the outer (material) person. In turn, the theories of our resurrection which we have reviewed are saying both too much and not enough. They say too much about the resurrection of the physical body; they say too little about the great miracle of transformation or re-creation that God will bring about in our resurrection.

Taking Paul as our guide, we can be confident that on our death we will experience resurrection. There will be no waiting; from an eschatological or eternal perspective, our death will coincide with "the End" of the space-time universe as we know it. Following the suggestion of C. F. D. Moule, all matter, including all the material of humankind, will return to the collective reservoir of the totality of matter, to be recreated by God in a miracle that will produce something new, including our new spirit-orientated bodies for our new existence.

It is the resurrection of Jesus that turns the conjecture into a conviction. Just as the risen body of Jesus was continuous with and connected with his earthly body, so will our resurrected body be connected with and continuous with our present bodies. But our bodies will be transformed. Like Christ, whose resurrection determines the nature of our life beyond the grave, our resurrection will involve being changed into a spiritual body. It is not the case that our resurrected body will consist in being a spirit.

Keeping in mind the contrasts between the earthly and resurrection body we listed earlier in this chapter, our new body will be so determined and motivated by the Spirit that it will exist in a way that enables our bodies – us – to live completely in the spiritual realm. Paul would say that, as a seed is discontinuous with but related to the plant, so will our resurrected bodies be related to but discontinuous with our earthly bodies. Our resurrected body will be a spirit-orientated body created by God to live in his presence.

Keeping in mind what Paul has said, our imperishability, immortality, glory, power and also the spiritual nature of our resurrected body is not something inherent in us. The resurrected body is a new action of creation – a creative gift of God for his people. In short, we anticipate a miracle on a scale familiar to us through the creation of the universe, the incarnation of God in Jesus, and the resurrection of Jesus.

For those of us who die before "the End", all this will take place "in the twinkling of an eye" at the moment of our death. But for those who are still alive up until "the End", it will appear that those who have died before us have been waiting until we join them to receive our new bodies. How God will do this – especially for, say, a stillborn baby or a physically handicapped person – can only be speculation. We will have to leave this matter in the hands of our loving Creator, who can be trusted.

## Notes

[1] See also, for example, Matthew 22:31/Luke 20:35; Acts 4:2; 17:32; 23:6; 24:21; 26:23; Hebrews 6:2; Revelation 2:10; 6:9–11; 20:4–6, 11–15.

[2] Compare, for example, 2 Clement 9:5; Shepherd of Hermas 5:6:5–7; Origen, Contra Celsum 2:43.

[3] See Wisdom of Solomon 3:4; 2 Maccabees 7:14 and also the book of Job.

[4] See Joel 2:1; Zephaniah 1:16; Revelation 11:15.

[5] John Donne, Holy Sonnets, vii.

[6] Justin Martyr, Resurrection 8; compare Irenaeus, Heresies 5.6.1; Origen, Principles 2:2:2; Jerome, To Pammachius 31.

[7] Justin Martyr, Resurrection 8; Athenagoras, Resurrection 15.

[8] On what follows see the more detailed discussion in Paul Badham, Christian Beliefs About Life After Death (London: SPCK, 1978), pp. 52–57.

[9] Compare Job 19:25–26; Isaiah 11; 40:5; 36:26–36; 37; Daniel 7:13–14.

[10] Compare 1 Corinthians 3:16; 1 Thessalonians 5:23.

[11] See Etienne Gilson, The Christian Philosophy of St. Thomas Aquinas (London: Gollancz, 1957), pp. 351–56.

[12] See Calvin, Institutes of the Christian Religion 3:6:3; 3:25:3 and David E. Holwerda, "Eschatology and History: A Look at Calvin's Eschatological Vision", in Donald K. McKim, ed., Readings in Calvin's Theology (Grand Rapids: Baker, 1984), p. 322.

[13] Augustine, City of God, 13:20; compare Justin Martyr, Resurrection 8; Origen, Principles 2:2:2; Augustine, Retractions 1:16.

[14] Norbert Wiener, The Human Use of Human Beings (London: Eyre and Spottiswoode, 1950), p. 109.

[15] Stephen T. Davis, "The Resurrection of the Dead", in Stephen T. Davis, ed., Death and Afterlife (London: Macmillan, 1989), pp. 119–44.

[16] For example, G. B. Caird, *The Truth of the Gospel* (London: Oxford University Press, 1950), p. 122.

[17] Alec R. Vidler, *A Plain Man's Guide to Christianity* (London: Heinemann, 1936), p. 248.

[18] See Paul Badham, *Christian Beliefs About Life After Death* (London: SPCK, 1978), pp. 86–87.

[19] C. F. D. Moule, "Introduction", in C. F. D. Moule, ed., *The Significance of the Resurrection for Faith in Jesus Christ* (London: SCM, 1968), p. 10.

# 6

## Do We Get a Second Chance?

---

If our life after death is determined the moment we die, death is a final and fearful thing if we are not prepared. Perhaps a loving God would give us a second chance beyond death. Especially troubling is what happens to babies after they die; those too young to be involved in deciding their future. Perhaps special arrangements are made for them. Perhaps we should be praying for our relatives and friends who have died, so that they are able to experience a positive life after death. Some people solve these problems by holding that there is such a place or state as purgatory as well as limbo, and that we should be praying for the dead. If we are to be thinking clearly about life after death, are these appropriate?

# Do We Get a Second Chance?

"I do not believe it would be possible to find any
joy that compares with that of a soul in purgatory,
except for the joy of the blessed in paradise"
Catherine of Genoa

"The Romish Doctrine concerning Purgatory . . . is
a fond thing vainly invented, and grounded upon no
warranty of Scripture, but rather repugnant to the
Word of God"
*Thirty-Nine Articles* of the Church of England

The American writer famous for the *Catch-22* novel was
lying paralyzed in his hospital bed fighting off sleep. Caught
in his own catch-22, Joseph Heller (1923–99), thought that if
he dozed off he might die like the others in the intensive care
ward. But if he did not sleep he might die anyway. Later he
said, "Yes. I was afraid to sleep. It was terrifying." Clare
Frances, the intrepid yachtswoman turned fiction writer, once
said, "The less of my life is left to lose, the more I cling to it."
The poet Dylan Thomas (1914–53) urged his dying father to
"Rage, rage against the dying of the light".

Even if death is only the subject of occasional, quiet whispers, it is the great fear of most of us. We fear the pain of the
death-bed, the separation from people, and the great unknown
beyond. Even if our death is sudden and painless, what if we
then must face the judgement of God? What if we should not
pass the judgement of God?

## Judgement: sooner or later?

As we have seen, Jesus is said to have told a story about a finely dressed, rich man who ate well and at whose gate there was a poor man named Lazarus. Both men died and must have immediately faced judgement, for the rich man is depicted as already in Hades and able to see across a vast chasm to the poor man, who is in heaven with Abraham (Luke 16:19–31).

As well as this so-called particular judgement of individuals when we die, a second public and general judgement is expected to await everyone on the Last Day. This general judgement is associated with the return of Christ: "the one ordained by God as the judge of the living and the dead" (Acts 10:42). From this the natural assumption is that we will be judged twice, first after we die and then in the Last Judgement. This apparent duplication or confusion over what happens to us as individuals when we die and what happens to all of us at "the End" has the same solution we found in the last chapter, when we are dealing with the timing of our resurrection. That is, when viewed from the perspective of this life, we are judged when we die; from the perspective of life after death (when there will be no time), our judgement takes place at "the End". In other words, the judgement we each face at death is the Last Judgement we all face on Christ's return.

## Judgement Day

The New Testament is clear that everyone is to face judgement (Acts 10:42; Romans 14:10–12). The basis of that judgement is also clear: it will be based on our relationship to Christ – or God through Christ (Luke 12:8–9). There are, however, places in the New Testament where the decision made on us in judgement will be determined by the things we have done (our "works", for example, Romans 2:6). Yet, it is not that we have to accomplish a certain number of good deeds to pass the test. Rather, the way we have lived will be the evidence of whether or not we have a life-changing relationship with Christ.

Thus the judgement we face will be a moment of division between those who are already truly in a relationship with Christ and those who do not have this relationship, each shown by the way they have lived. When seen in this way, judgement will have already taken place in this life when we enter into a relationship with Christ (compare John 3:19–20). But what about those of us who have never had an opportunity to have this relationship?

## A second chance?

Once, when we were flying into Adelaide airport in South Australia, among those meeting us was a couple keen to show us Andrew, their three-month-old son. What a joy to see him! A few nights later his mother, Susan, found him, very pale. Andrew was dead. His death was a "cot death". What happens to babies when they die? If they are unbaptized, are they barred from heaven? If they die too young to have been able to respond to God's love for them, are they denied a full and positive after-life?

Then, what about adults? Do they get a second chance after death? Indeed, how could a good God condemn us to hell if we had not had a reasonable opportunity to know him and prepare for death? Would not a good God give us a chance after death to be prepared for eternity? Also, if people are given a second chance, should we pray for them after they have died? Attempting to answer questions like these has given rise to the ideas of purgatory, limbo and praying for the dead.

## Purgatory

Purgatory is said to be the intermediate state between this life and eternal life. It is not a place of trial or judgement. Those who are thought to go to purgatory are said to be on their way to heaven. Their decisions and lives on this earth have destined them for eternal life. Nevertheless, through some kind of purifying (that is, purgatorial) pain, they make expiation for light (or venial), unforgiven sins. They also receive punishment for sins already forgiven. Purgatory is also said to free people from the inclination to sin.

The awareness of having already attained salvation and knowing that nothing can imperil their final happiness means that undergoing purgatory in order to be perfected and prepared for final union with God is an intense joy. This is why Catherine of Genoa (1447–1510) can say, "I do not believe it would be possible to find any joy that compares with that of a soul in purgatory, except for the joy of the blessed in paradise." Then, having been perfected, souls are able to enter heaven.

This doctrine of purgatory presumes there is a difference between mortal sin and venial or light sin. (Mortal sins are said to cause the eternal loss of the soul; venial or light sins do not lead to eternal damnation.) It is also presumed that, while the guilt may be forgiven in this life, the punishment due to sin is not always and necessarily forgiven. Thus the punishment must be paid for in this or the future life.

It is agreed by those who believe in purgatory that since punishment will cease with the Last Judgement, purgatorial punishment is temporary. Yet it is impossible to determine how long the punishment will last, for purgatory is outside time.

There is less certainty in the documents of the church when we inquire about the nature of purgatory, save that there will be some kind of purifying punishment involving real spiritual sorrows, such as affliction, sadness, chagrin and shame. The most basic and profound suffering handed out in purgatory is thought to be the temporary denial of seeing heaven – the beatific vision. Some think there needs to be other punishment to prepare the soul for heaven. This punishment is traditionally taken to be a real fire. (The Greek word for fire is *pur*, from which "purgatory" comes.) However, some argue that a real fire could have no impact on a soul.

Purgatory was rejected by the Reformers, is abhorred by many contemporary Protestants and was never accepted by the Eastern church. Yet the idea of purgatory has had a long and illustrious history.

Although the doctrine of purgatory as we know it today did not come into existence until the twelfth century, elements of it can be traced back even to before the early church. What can be found as early as Plato is expressed poetically by Virgil (70–19 BC), when he says that, after we die, we are ceaselessly schooled by retribution, and pay in punishment for our old offences. Some of us, he says, are hung for the wind to blow us clean, while others more wicked are washed in deep water or have evil burnt out of them (*The Aeneid* 6:735–47).

The first Christian to express the idea that some sort of "compensatory discipline" may await some of us in the afterlife was Tertullian (c. 160–c. 220), the renowned north African theologian and priest of Carthage. Clement of Alexandria (c. 150–c. 215) also considered the possibility of there being "saving discipline" and a "discriminating fire" which could purify, educate and sanctify the souls of those not beyond correction.[1] The idea of purgatory was developed and became popular through the *Dialogues* of Pope Gregory the Great (c. 540–604). He said that a purging fire will cleanse the soul from minor faults before judgement and that the prayers of others and the sacrifice of the mass can free a soul (4:40–41; 4:60:1).

Saint Augustine, on whom Gregory was relying, has been

so immensely influential in shaping a thousand years of Western theology that what he says on the subject remains important. Reflecting on Malachi 3:1–6, Isaiah 4:4 and especially 1 Corinthians 3:10–15, where Paul says that on "the Day" fire will test the work of each person, Augustine says that it seems clear that in the last judgement there are to be purgatorial pains handed out to some of the faithful. Augustine even lays down rules for the use of "suffrages", as prayers and alms offered for the dead were called. The first rule was that prayers for the dead did not benefit all the dead; it was too late for the damned, and those already in heaven did not need them. The second rule was that a person only benefited from prayer if they earned such merit while they were alive.[2] With the passing of time, these rules became the basis of charitable works, giving rise to prayer houses and charitable institutions.

It was Thomas Aquinas who produced the classic formulation of purgatory. He said that, in purgatory, suffering takes place for unforgiven guilt for light or venial sins, and punishment for remaining mortal and venial sins is met at the point of death (*Summa Theologiae* IIIa, q.69, a.2). This suffering – more painful than the greatest pain in this life and caused by actual fire – varies with the measure of guilt. The pain is accepted voluntarily, the sinner knowing it is the last stage of preparation for heaven. Aquinas taught that for an unbaptized child there is no pain, only the loss of blessedness reserved for the baptized. Aquinas admitted that neither the Bible nor reason enables us to locate purgatory.

## *Purgatory in Dante's* Divine Comedy

Aquinas was followed not least by the Italian poet Alighieri Dante (1265–1321) in his sacred and graphic poem *The Divine Comedy*, which he completed in 1321. Dante depicted purgatory, with its various parts, as a mountain reaching up to heaven.

Ante-purgatory, probably Dante's invention, consists of two terraces forming the lower reaches of the mountain, where those who died failing to take advantage of the means of grace have to wait before being admitted to purgatory. Peter's gate into purgatory is approached by three steps: confession, contrition and satisfaction. Ascending the mountain, there are seven cornices devoted to the purging of the seven capital sins. In lower purgatory perverted love is dealt with: pride, envy and anger. In middle purgatory defective love or sloth is dealt with, leaving upper purgatory for excessive love of secondary good as the focus of attention: coveting, gluttony and lust. On every cornice the discipline follows the same pattern. There is a penance appropriate to the sin (either the patient endurance of the sin and its effects, or the practice of the opposing virtue, or both). There is a meditation of the whip and the bridle. There is a prayer taken from the Psalms, or a hymn, and a benediction taken from the beatitudes. Finally, the angel assigned to the cornice erases the brand of the sin from the soul's forehead and directs the soul upwards by the Pass of Pardon. The desire of heaven makes souls fly towards God. This causes the mountain to tremble constantly, with a joyful thunderclap marking the arrival of each soul into paradise.

But not all images of purgatory are so congenial. Nor is the idea of purgatory everywhere accepted. Views relating to purgatory were a matter of individual opinion until the Council of Florence in 1439. There the doctrine was stamped with the authority of the church. However, hopes of reconciling the two major wings of the church in this council were not met. The churches of the East objected to the idea of a literal fire and to the distinction the West was making between guilt and punishment.

*Purgatory and the Reformers*

Some of the Reformers were ambivalent about purgatory. For

example, in the *Ninety-five Theses*, which he posted on the door of the castle church of Wittenberg on 31 October 1517, Luther assumes the existence of purgatory and that prayer for the dead can release departed souls from their misery. Yet in his *Schmalkaldic Articles* (1537) he says that purgatory is to be regarded as nothing other than an illusion of the devil and discarded as error and idolatry. He came to this conclusion because the idea of purgatory being able to help souls is contrary to the fundamental article that Christ alone can help us. He adds that Saint Augustine, who left open the question of the existence of purgatory, offered no scriptural support for it (2:2:12–13), a view maintained in Lutheranism (compare *Book of Concord*). Nevertheless, the Council of Trent issued a decree (3–4 December 1563) stating "that purgatory exists, and that the souls detained there are helped by the prayers of the faithful and most of all by the acceptable sacrifice of the altar."

At the same time that Luther was at odds with the church in Germany, the Church of England was drawing up its *Thirty-nine Articles*, which eventually became binding on the clergy in 1571. Article 22 is unequivocal: "The Romish Doctrine concerning Purgatory . . . is a fond thing vainly invented, and grounded upon no warranty of Scripture, but rather repugnant to the Word of God."

Calvin entertained no doubts about purgatory. He put it forcefully that the doctrine was constructed out of many blasphemies and was "a deadly fiction of Satan, which nullifies the cross of Christ, inflicts unbearable contempt upon God's mercy, and overturns and destroys our faith" (*Institutes of the Christian Religion* 3:5:6).

## Purgatory for Catholics and Protestants

As we will see in a moment, prayer for the dead remains popular, especially among Roman Catholic people. But in Catholic theological writings there has been a diminution of interest in purgatory; Vatican II does not mention it, for example. And in the 22 volumes of *Theological Investigations* by the prolific Jesuit theologian Karl Rahner (1904–84) it is rarely and only briefly mentioned. Referring to the tradition of the church, not Scripture, Rahner says purgatory is a place needed for the individual, between death and entering heaven. Purgatory is for the payment of the debts of punishment due to sin, and a place where the basic decision and disposition of a person permeates the whole person (for example, 3:153, 203; 19:181–93).

When we turn to the work of some Protestants, we find there is an increasing interest in purgatory. Indeed, John Hick considers that a rehabilitation of the idea is much to be desired. He considers that the basic concept of purgatory – as a period between this life and our ultimate state – seems unavoidable. He says that, with the idea of purgatory, the gap is bridged between our lack of perfection at the end of this life and the perfection of the heavenly state in which we are to participate. Purgatory, he says, is simply the name given in Roman Catholic theology to this bridge.[3] As logical as this seems, we need to discuss it further, for it seems to fly in the face of clear biblical teaching.

## Purgatory: an assessment

In order to support the view that when we die we go to a place to be purified and made ready for heaven, a number of cases have been made for purgatory.

### Case 1

It is clear that we are not morally perfect when we die. Well we might say with Leonardo Da Vinci (1452–1519), "I have offended God and mankind because my work did not reach the quality it should have." Or, contemplating our fate, we could echo the last words of the Anglo-Irish dramatist,

Richard Sheridan (1751-1816): "I am absolutely undone." Yet, in heaven we anticipate being in a state of complete moral perfection. Therefore, for us to enter heaven, either there must be an instantaneous and abrupt transition between our present state and that which will enable us to enter heaven, or there must be an intermediate state where we are prepared for heaven. Since an instantaneous transition or change in us is inconceivable (so the argument goes), there must be an intermediate state of purgatory.[4]

But is such an abrupt change so inconceivable? If people can be changed instantaneously, purgatory would be unnecessary. We might argue that instantaneous religious conversions are examples showing that God can change someone abruptly. But we would probably have to concede that what appears to be an instantaneous conversion had a time of preparation, and, subsequently, there was a significant period of time when old habits were being altered before the person reached their present "changed" life.

Nevertheless, looking at this problem from another perspective, the abrupt change is quite conceivable. If we understand our after-life to be timeless, our whole future life will be instantly and simultaneously present for us and God. To put it differently (and perhaps more simply!), from our perspective here in time, an instantaneous change can take place when we die, because it will be all eternity taking place in the moment of death!

There is another and more important perspective that helps us see that we can expect to be changed instantly when we die. Indeed, to talk about our ineligibility to enter heaven when we die is to miss a (or the) central theme in the Bible regarding the nature of our salvation.

It is true that, when we receive or enter salvation, the Holy Spirit begins to make profound changes in us. It is also true that, through our life and generally with our cooperation, the Holy Spirit goes on changing us into the likeness of the perfect Jesus. Further, it is also true that this process is not complete when we die. However, it is equally true that, by God's grace or unmerited kindness, we are instantly given a status before God that enables us to be in his company both now and when we die (Romans 5:1–2).

We can conclude that our lack of perfection is not, in fact, a hindrance for our entering heaven. Out of his love God gives us the necessary righteousness, and (to recall our last point) at death we are no longer bound by the impediments of time. In the moment of all eternity we can be changed.

### Case 2

There is a second case for purgatory which we need to take into account. It is said that, if we are instantly changed to be fit for heaven, the person we become will be so different from what we are, that we will not be the same person. Therefore, so the argument goes, purgatory is needed as a place of transition for us.

There are a number of responses we can make to this argument. In the first place, we can keep in mind what we have just said: from our perspective an instantaneous transition is timeless in our after-life. Also, it could be said that there might be the kind of moral change in us that would mean we were not the same person. However, our memories would provide the link between our present life and our future life so that we would know ourselves to be the same person. In any case, whether we are instantly or gradually changed, if we are changed, purgatory does not offer a solution to the problem of "not being the same person". Then, further, it is the conviction of biblical writers that what we shall be and experience in the after-life is already, in part, what we are and what is part of our experience, albeit in an attenuated and proleptic fashion. Therefore, in the light of our present experience of God and his work in our present life, our future life will be a glorious continuation of it.

*Case 3*

Still a third point could be put forward for the existence of purgatory. It is a moral argument. It is agreed that God has created us with a free will, for he desires us to make a free response to him. However, if we die imperfect, yet enter a heaven where we are perfect, we have been denied our free will in taking part in completing our readiness for heaven. Therefore, there must be a place of purgatory or preparation where we can continue being involved in freely responding to God in our preparation for heaven. To this point we can also reply that, beyond death, we are not dealing with the constraints of time known to us now. Without any compromise to God's grace or our freedom, the choice we make in this life in relation to God's grace is not violated but able to be realized in an instant.

Although I am making much of the idea of the timelessness of the after-life, it has to be conceded that there are those who say such a concept is incoherent.[5] It is said, for example, that if God were timeless or outside the processes we know, he would be lifeless.[6] The prolific Swiss Protestant theologian Karl Barth (1886–1968), put it strongly in saying that, "Without God's complete temporality the content of the Christian message has no shape."[7] But, this is not convincing. At the risk of trivializing the philosophical debates about the possibility of an unchanging eternal God knowing and being involved in time, we can say that we can readily imagine that the sphere of God can be both without spacial limit and time, yet, at the same time, we can imagine that God is able to be involved in our world of space and time. Indeed, the idea of the incarnation depends on it.

*Purgatory and the Bible*

Any light the Bible sheds on purgatory is of particular interest to us in our attempt to think clearly about life after death.

There are two texts in the New Testament and one in the Old Testament apocrypha that need our attention.

In 1 Corinthians 3:13–15 Paul says that on "the Day" a fire will test the work of each person. Even if the work is burned up, the builder will be saved, but only as one escaping "as it were" through fire. Since the time of Origen, this has been seen as support for the idea of the purifying fire of purgatory. However, this is far from Paul's intention. In using the phrase "as it were" (3:15), Paul is intending a metaphor for fire, nothing more. Paul's point is that the Day (of Judgement) is like a fire (also see 2 Thessalonians 1:8) and that a person caught even in a badly built house will escape only as one saved from a burning building. There is no hint in this text of a fire purifying the person.

In 2 Timothy 1:18 the writer asks for "mercy from the Lord on that day" for Onesiphorus. The assumption of those who look to this verse for evidence of purgatory is that Onesiphorus is dead and this is a prayer for the dead. As we will see at the end of this chapter when we deal with prayers for the dead, this is an unwarranted assumption and a forced interpretation of the text.

Turning back to the Old Testament for scriptural support for the doctrine of purgatory, the only passage to hand is one from the apocrypha, 2 Maccabees 12:44–45, where Judas is said to offer sacrifices and to pray for the dead to be freed from their sin. For Protestants this passage is of little consequence, for it lies outside their canon of Scripture. But for the Orthodox and Roman Catholics, it is part of their Bible and requires attention.

Nevertheless, we have to leave this passage aside. As was the expectation of the time (compare Daniel 12:1–3), Judas was most probably regarding his prayers as necessary for the general (eschatological) resurrection rather than for a personal, purifying period between death and entering heaven.

It may be comforting for some people to imagine a kindly

God allowing people a second post-mortem opportunity, either to be accepted into his presence if they so wish, or to be so changed that they are fit for heaven. But we have to conclude that such a concept is both unnecessary and dishonouring to the sufficiency of the work of Christ, as well as contrary to the teaching of the Bible. As harsh as Calvin may sound, he is probably right to say that "purgatory is simply a dreadful blasphemy against Christ" for it "nullifies the cross of Christ, inflicts unbearable contempt upon God's mercy, and overturns and destroys our faith" (*Institutes of the Christian Religion* 3:5:6).

Not only does the Bible say nothing explicit about the existence of purgatory: Paul, for example, says that the change which God brings to a person who is "in Christ" is both profound and instantaneous. Further, in speaking about how we are to be able to enter God's presence (or the kingdom of God, 1 Corinthians 15:50), Paul explicitly states that we shall be changed in the twinkling of an eye (15:52). Therefore, our present moral imperfections are no impediment to inheriting the kingdom of God (15:50), because of the work of Christ on our behalf. If Calvin's view is harsh, in the light of what the Bible says, we can retreat no further than to say that purgatory is an unnecessary doctrine.

## Limbo

What happens to babies when they die? Since baptism is important to some people, they will want to know what happens after death to those babies or adults who have never been baptized. Even those who do not see baptism as being of such significance might still ask about the post-mortem destiny of those too young to commit sin knowingly. Then, do those who are too intellectually disabled to understand these issues have the opportunity of a positive life after death? There is also the interesting question of what happened to the so-called saints of the Old Testament who lived before Christ and who were, it is suggested, liberated by him when, according to the *Apostles' Creed*, "he descended into hell" (compare 1 Peter 4:6). It cannot be, so it is argued, that these people are to be excluded from heaven. Nor, surely, can it be that they will suffer in hell.

The answer to these questions that developed in the ancient church and has been maintained in the Roman Catholic Church is to say that there is a state of limbo, from the Latin *limbus*, meaning "hem" or "edge". Using a term coined by Albertus Magnus (c. 1200–1280), the German bishop and philosopher, there is supposed to be a *limbus infantium* for infants and a *limbus patrum* for the Old Testament patriarchs. In *The Divine Comedy*, Dante even proposed a limbo for such greats as Socrates, Plato and Virgil.

Limbo was a place and state for the dead who were neither in heaven, nor in hell, nor in purgatory. The theory is that, while children may be innocent of personal sin, they are still in a state of original sin, so they remain in limbo for eternity. Of course, since Christ has descended to hell and transported the Old Testament saints to heaven, *limbus patrum* has thereafter been unoccupied.

Neither the Bible nor the theologians of the first few centuries dealt specifically with the most pressing issue of what happened to innocent children or the unbaptized. When the issue was discussed, the early church fathers were generally lenient. For example, the theologian Saint Gregory of Nyssa took the view that unbaptized babies neither suffered the torments of hell nor entered the bliss of heaven. In line with the teaching of the Bible, a positive after-life was available to all who belonged to Christ.

Pelagius (c. 360–c. 420), a British lay monk who settled in Rome, also maintained that God does not withhold eternal life from unbaptized infants, but neither does he grant them access to heaven. That is, the unbaptized young are in a state of innocence rather than being damned, and so have a measure of happiness.

As a result of the debate between Pelagius and Augustine, Pelagianism was eventually deemed heretical at the Council of Carthage on 1 May 418. Thereafter, Augustine's view prevailed, that all who died without being baptized, and therefore still being in original sin, were condemned to hell. However, Augustine granted that they only suffered some mild degree of punishment compared to adults. In any case, argued Augustine, such punishment was better than complete annihilation.

Saint Augustine's views held sway at least until the time of the philosopher–theologian Peter Abelard (1079–1142/3) and Peter Lombard (c. 1100–1160), who became bishop of Paris the year before he died. Against what were thought to be the excessive views of Augustine, Abelard stated that unbaptized babies only suffered the grief of separation from God, not the full pains of hell. Similarly, Lombard, whose *Four Books of Sentences* became widely known and influential, especially as a student textbook, agreed that infants who died without being baptized suffered "darkness", not hell itself.

Just what kind of life is expected in *limbus* is unclear. Thomas Aquinas said that people in limbo enjoyed full and natural happiness. He took this line based on the view that original sin was not a positive fault but a privation. Therefore, as it would be unreasonable for God to punish positively something that was not a positive fault, punishment through the experience of pain would be unreasonable. Here, Thomas was following Bonaventure in distinguishing between hell and limbo. Limbo, which was neither joyful nor sad, was for children with whom God had established a relationship of unchanging love and knowledge. Since Aquinas, the issue of whether or not we ought to believe in a limbo has been questioned by many theologians but, officially, remains untouched by the Roman Catholic Church.

## Limbo: an assessment

What are we to make of the idea of a state or place of limbo? We have already noted that this is an important question for some, not least because it has implications for what they understand happens to children who die unbaptized or too young to have been able to respond to God's love, and who have not made any personal choices to deserve the punishment of hell.

Assuming baptism is necessary for salvation, a novel solution to this problem is to interpret baptism to include those who have not actually been through the usual sacrament of baptism. Thus Aquinas developed two categories of baptism: one of blood and one of desire. Others have gone so far as to understand baptism in a way that includes everyone, by seeing death as a sacrament from which the saving power of baptism arises.[8] But these solutions stretch the imagination more than solve the problem as to whether or not we should believe in limbo. A more helpful way forward is to determine whether or not baptism is necessary for salvation.

The clearest statement in the Bible that baptism is to be thought necessary for salvation is Acts 2:38: "Repent and be baptised . . . so that your sins may be forgiven; and you will receive the gift of the Holy Spirit." However, a close reading of what Luke says in his gospel and in Acts suggests that salvation is to be linked to repentance, with baptism as the medium through which repentance is expressed.[9] This means that, taking our perspective from a point where the Bible is clearest about the necessity of baptism, we can conclude that baptism is irrelevant to the question of the existence of limbo: the unbaptized can be saved.

A popular way of dispensing with the idea of limbo is to argue that a good God would not exclude the innocent from his heaven. But, at least from a biblical perspective, no one is innocent. For example, in Romans 1:18–2:20 Paul goes to considerable lengths to make this point, so that from Paul's perspective limbo would be unnecessary, for one is either saved or not saved.

In any case, limbo has to be dispensed with for a number of clear reasons. First, postulating the existence of limbo does not offer a solution to the problem of what happens to the young or innocent if they are not deserving of hell. To say that the young or innocent are in limbo is, in fact, still to exclude them from heaven. In the case of those too young to respond to God's love, I would want to argue that we are at the mercy of a loving God for their eternal destination. We have no alternative other than to leave the matter in the hands of a God we have come to trust as fully just and totally loving.

Secondly, limbo is unnecessary because, at the moment of death, whether we are a child or an adult, we are awakened to our full spiritual, eternal potential. All of us, at death, have complete knowledge that develops in a single moment into an eternal state (see 1 Corinthians 15:52). This would mean that none of us dies as a child. The objection that is brought against this view is that it empties the present life of its religious significance, but this objection has no force. Any other view denigrates God's work in a child and inflates the value of an adult life as able to prepare us for the after-life without the intervening love of God.

Thirdly, we can dispense with the idea of limbo because there is no mention of it in the Bible. Indeed, no one has tried to defend it from this perspective.

## Prayers for the dead

I have just had the moving experience of visiting some of the catacombs near the Appian Way on the outskirts of old Rome. There, in ancient times, Christians not only buried their dead but returned to worship and to scratch on the wall their prayers for their beloved departed.

Those who believe in prayers for the dead frequently note that, when his mother, Saint Monica, died, Saint Augustine offered prayers for the repose of her soul. In his *Confessions* he says: "I now pray for my mother's sins . . . Forgive them, Lord, forgive them . . . Let no one wrest her from your protection . . . her debts have been remitted by him [Jesus]" (9:13; compare *Enchiridion* 69–70).

Also, holding to the value of praying for the dead is closely associated with a belief in purgatory and is based on the view that there are those who have died who have not yet reached their heavenly destination. These can be helped by our praying. From inscriptions in the catacombs in Rome we can see that praying for the dead was a very early Christian practice. So important was this practice that not only do we find it supported by Tertullian and Cyprian, for example, but also that one of the charges against the fourth century heretic Arius of Pontus was that he denied the value of praying for the dead.

Aquinas thought that Christ's descent into hell, affirmed in the *Apostles' Creed*, set us the example of love, to come to the assistance of our friends who are in purgatory. In his exposition of the *Apostles' Creed* Aquinas said that, according to tradition, there were three main deeds that brought relief to the dead: masses, prayers and alms. Aquinas added fasting as a fourth deed.[10]

In the Roman Catholic Church, praying for the dead was reaffirmed in the Council of Trent (1545–63). Scriptural support was found in 2 Maccabees 12:40–46, which we have already noted in the context of discussing purgatory. Verse 44 says: "If he [Judas] were not expecting that those who had fallen would rise again, it would have been superfluous and foolish to pray for the dead." The Protestant Reformers also prayed for the dead. However, they eventually came to denounce the practice. In rejecting the doctrine of purgatory, as well as 2 Maccabees, along with the rest of the apocrypha, from Scripture, the Reformers could not see prayers for the dead clearly supported in the Bible.

For the Anglican churches the 1552 revision of *The Book of Common Prayer* brought to an end any possibility of official prayers for the dead. No dirges or devout prayers were to be sung or said for the departed. One of the homilies published in 1562–63 during the reign of Elizabeth I to help raise the standard of preaching was "An Homilie Or Sermon Concerning Prayer". It implores the hearer not to "let us dreame any more, that the soules of the dead are any thing at all holpen by our prayers." Instead the homily is firm in saying that "the soule of man passing out of the body, goeth straight wayes either to heaven, or else to hell, whereof the one needeth no prayer, and the other is without redemption." However, not everyone, including Hugh Latimer (c. 1485–1555), was hostile to the idea of praying for the dead. Nevertheless, considerable controversy surrounded the introduction of a thanksgiving for the departed in the 1662 Prayer Book.

In the 20th century, prayers for the dead became increasingly common. The Scottish Episcopal church adopted prayers for the dead into its liturgy in 1912. In 1928 the Protestant Episcopal church followed suit.

In the Lambeth Report of 1958 the bishops said that, although Scripture had often been quoted both for and against the practice of prayers for the dead, the evidence was not conclusive either way. However, they were adamant that Scripture and the documents of their church did not allow them to condone practices and prayers for the dead which would reflect the false doctrines of purgatory, which they noted were condemned by the church at the Reformation. On the other hand, they recognized that, so far as prayers for the dead were an expression of the love that united members of the mystical body of Christ, the majority of Anglicans were quite sure that death did not remove the need for and appropriateness of praying for the dead that God would fulfil his perfect will in them. The bishops also recognized that more conservative, evangelical Anglicans were content to think of Christians who died as having immediately entered into "joy and felicity". Expressing the spirit of the age, the bishops concluded that there was room for both points of view (2:92–93).

Yet, large sections of the Christian church remain unconvinced and reject prayers for the dead principally on the grounds that they are unscriptural. Two passages in particular come under discussion when seeking support in the Bible for prayers for the dead: 2 Timothy 1:16–18 and 1 John 5:16–17.

The writer of 2 Timothy 1:18 says, "may the Lord grant that he [Onesiphorus] will find mercy from the Lord on that day". This passage is thought to be a proof-text for prayers for the dead on the grounds that Onesiphorus is assumed to be dead. This assumption is made because only his family is mentioned in this passage and in 4:19. However, even if Onesiphorus is dead, the writer is not praying for Onesiphorus but simply expressing a hope to his readers: "may the Lord grant that he will find mercy from the Lord on that day!" (1:18). More pertinently, prayers for the dead are not in view in this passage. Therefore it would be unwise to use such an uncertain base for what is, on other grounds, a questionable practice.

So far as 1 John 5:16-17 is relevant to praying for the dead, it is a discouragement to the practice. The writer says: "There is sin that is mortal; I do not say that you should pray about that." Here John is discouraging prayer for any believer who has experienced divine judgement in the form of death. So, that prayer for the dead would be against God's will.

## Results?

The results of this chapter are not encouraging for those who are expecting a second chance after death to decide about their so-called eternal destiny. We have seen that the ideas of purgatory and limbo are neither necessary nor supported from a biblical perspective. More seriously, we can conclude that the ideas of purgatory and limbo are an insult to the care of a loving God for his people. These ideas also mock the power of God to fit us – in an instant – for communion with him, as well as being an affront to the sufficiency of the preparatory work of Christ. Of course, if there is no purgatory nor limbo, praying for the dead is superfluous. Nevertheless, while making no difference to the person's life, prayers for the dead can be an expression and celebration of "the communion of saints", a source of comfort for those who remain in this life.

## Notes

[1] Tertullian, *De Anima* xxxv; Clement of Alexandria, *Stomata* 4:24; 7:6, 10; compare Origen, *Principles* 2:10:4–6; Basil, *Homily* 11:2.

[2] Augustine, *City of God* 20:25; compare 21:26; *Enchiridion* 110, see also 68.

[3] John Hick, *Death and Eternal Life* (Louisville, KY: Westminster/John Knox, 1994), p. 202.

[4] See David Brown, "No Heaven Without Purgatory", *Religious Studies* 21 (4, 1985), p. 447.

[5] For example, Anthony Kenny, *The God of the Philosophers* (Oxford: Clarendon, 1979), pp. 38–48.

[6] Compare, for example, Paul Tillich, *Systematic Theology*, 3 vols. (Digswell Place, UK: James Nisbet, 1953, 1957, 1964), 1: 305.

[7] Karl Barth, *Church Dogmatics*, II.I (Edinburgh: T & T Clark, 1957), p. 620.

[8] Bruno Webb, "Unbaptized Infants and the Quasi-Sacrament of Death", *The Downside Review* 71 (No. 225, Summer 1953), pp. 243–57.

[9] See Luke 3:3, 8; 24:47; Acts 3:19; 5:31 and James D. G. Dunn, *The Acts of the Apostles* (London: Epworth, 1996), p. 33.

[10] Thomas Gilby, *St. Thomas Aquinas: Theological Texts* (London: Oxford University Press, 1955), p. 264.

# 7

## Can a Good God Condemn Some of Us to Hell?

Most people are familiar with the traditional view of hell as "a great furnace of wrath, a wide and bottomless pit, full of the fire of wrath", as Jonathan Edwards put it. But not everyone is happy with this dreadful destiny that God has for some people. Surely a loving God would see that everyone, in the end, is saved. Others propose a compromise: heaven for the just, annihilation for the rest. The difficulty in thinking clearly about these issues is not only that equally great minds have taken different sides, but that the Bible has been used as an ally for all views.

# Can a Good God Condemn Some of Us to Hell?

"O sinner! Consider the fearful danger you are in"
Jonathan Edwards

"Beware of new and strange doctrines about hell
and the eternity of punishment"
Bishop J. C. Ryle

If good people – or however we may describe them – have a blissful after-life with God or are in heaven, what happens to "the rest"? Islam teaches that, after we die, in order for our soul to get to paradise it must pass along a narrow bridge over hell, a huge crater of fire beneath. The damned fall from the bridge and suffer torments, unless Allah (God) decides otherwise. For Hindus, hell is only one stage in the life of the soul. As all our actions have consequences and because of reincarnation (see chapter 3), the time spent in one or more of the 21 hells under the netherworld is of no final significance. The Jaina hell (*bhumis*) is a place where demons torture sinners until any evil accumulated during their lives has been exhausted. For Buddhists, who deny the existence of both the individual and the world soul, multiple hells correspond to *karmavacara*, the cosmic realm in which the five senses may be experienced in a variety of bodies and perceptions.

The Christian view of hell is less clear than is at first thought. In a now-famous sermon called "Sinners in the Hands of An Angry God", Jonathan Edwards (1703–58), the American Congregational theologian and philosopher, was certain and graphic in his description of what happens to the unrepentant:

The God that holds you over the pit of hell, much as one holds a spider, or some loathsome insect over the fire, abhors you, and is dreadfully provoked: his wrath towards you burns like fire; he looks upon you as worthy of nothing else, but to be cast into the fire; he is of purer eyes than to bear to have you in his sight; you are ten thousand times more abominable in his eyes, than the most hateful venomous serpent is in ours . . .

O sinner! Consider the fearful danger you are in: it is a great furnace of wrath, a wide and bottomless pit, full of the fire of wrath, that you are held over in the hand of that God, whose wrath is provoked and incensed as much against you, as against many of the damned in hell.

This striking version of the view that the wicked suffer eternal punishment or suffer "unending physical torment", as Augustine put it,[1] is only one of three broad views which have been in circulation since the early days of the church. A second view, known as universalism, holds that everyone, including the wicked, are eventually saved. The third view is that the wicked are annihilated, salvation or life after death only being conditional. As each view is still firmly held, supposedly supported by biblical data, we need to examine each of them, to come to our own conclusion as to which is the most faithful to a Christianity attempting to reflect a biblical trajectory.

## 1. Eternal punishment in hell

The most famous early advocate of the traditional view of hell, reflected in Edwards' sermon which has just been quoted, was Saint Augustine. Following Plato, he simply took for granted that our soul was immortal by nature.

Augustine relied mainly on the story of the separation of the sheep and the goats (Matthew 25:31–46) in holding that some people would undergo an everlasting process of suffering of body and soul (*City of God* 6:12; 21:9–10). With

Augustine being held in such high regard throughout the history of the Western church, his views of eternal bliss for some and eternal damnation for others have dominated the church.

In the early church it was believed that hell was located in the centre of the earth. It was assumed that the damned would burn there for ever without being consumed for, as Augustine noted, for example, the fires of volcanoes burn continuously without being consumed. Adding to the horrors of hell and the pleasure of those in heaven was the idea that the saints in heaven could see and even enjoy the suffering in hell.[2]

Later speculations about the gruesome details of hell were fuelled by Dante's *The Divine Comedy*. Writing between 1310 and 1314, Dante describes a place of total terror where sinners writhe and scream as they boil in blood and run naked and terrified from hordes of biting snakes in a land of darkness and dense fog. The claustrophobic nightmare of the damned is to be trapped for ever in lead cloaks and to endure thick, burning smoke charring their nostrils.

A little nearer to our own time, E. B. Pusey (1800–1882), one of the leaders of the Oxford Movement, reflected the literal and graphic understanding of hell in a book he wrote near the end of his life, *What is of Faith as to Everlasting Punishment?* Pusey said: "You know the fierce, intense, burning heat of a furnace, how it consumes in a moment anything cast into it. Its misery to the damned shall be that they feel it, but can't be consumed by it. The fire shall pierce them, penetrate them; it shall be, Scripture says, like a molten 'lake of fire', rolling, tossing, immersing, but not destroying."[3] And the famous Baptist preacher Charles Spurgeon (1834–1892) of the Metropolitan Tabernacle in New Park Street Chapel in Southwark, London offered an equally gruesome image of hell. He said, "in fire exactly like that which we have on earth thy body will lie, asbestos-like, forever unconsumed, all thy veins roads for the feet of Pain to travel on, every nerve a string on which the Devil shall forever play his diabolical tune of hell's unutterable lament."[4]

While forgoing the graphic images of former times, there are still strong advocates of the view that the wicked are destined to be punished for ever. For example, Leon L. Morris (b. 1914), the Australian New Testament scholar and one-time principal of Ridley College, Melbourne, has written that, "If we are to be true to the whole teaching of Scripture, we must come to the conclusion that the ultimate fate of the wicked is eternal punishment, though we must add that we have no way of knowing in exactly what that punishment consists."[5]

Not surprisingly, numerous problems have been raised against this traditional view, some of which we have already encountered in previous chapters.[6]

1. Eternal and conscious punishment by a God of love is argued to be logically inconsistent.
2. God's justice would be put into question if he forever punished some people. That is, it is inconceivable that mere human beings – over a brief three score years and ten – should require everlasting punishment for anything they could do.
3. The view that some remain in punishment forever brings into question God's supposed ability to be ultimately victorious over sin and able to win all his creatures with his love. In other words, the view that he is to be victorious over his people cannot be reconciled with the view that he will forever punish some of them.
4. It is often suggested that the language of destruction, so widespread in both Old Testament and New Testament, is not taken sufficiently seriously in the traditional view. That is, those who hold this view mistake the eternal or everlasting consequences of God's annihilating or destroying judgement with its everlasting duration.
5. It is said that the view that some are damned forever

depends on Greek philosophy, which sees human beings as naturally immortal, a view we have seen is foreign to the Bible.

In short, on the doctrine of hell, many would say with C. S. Lewis (1898–1963): "There is no doctrine which I would more willingly remove from Christianity than this, if it lay in my power . . . I would pay any price to be able to say truthfully, 'All will be saved'."[7]

## The New Testament and eternal punishment

Not only are there the problems we have just listed, but when we turn to the New Testament we are faced with difficulties in maintaining the traditional view that some people are punished in hell forever.

### Punishment without end

There are some passages in the Bible that obviously support the traditional view of everlasting punishment in hell for some. The clearest passage is in the last book of the New Testament where it is said that those who worship the beast – that is, the anti-Christian powers – will be tormented with fire, the smoke of their torment going up forever and ever: "There is no rest day or night for those who worship the beast" (Revelation 14:11). Revelation 20:10 is equally clear and graphic on the fate of the wicked: "they will be tormented day and night forever and ever" (compare 20:15).

In the synoptic gospels there are three passages which deserve our attention where Jesus clearly sets out the idea of eternal punishment. First, there is a passage where Jesus is said to talk about eternal punishment in a section of Mark on how to be a follower of Jesus. Mark has some graphic sayings of Jesus which show starkly the importance and cost of "entering life". Jesus says: "it is better for you to enter the kingdom of God with one eye than to have two eyes and to be thrown into hell, where their worm never dies, and the fire is never quenched" (Mark 9:43–48).

Those who want to argue against eternal punishment take this passage to mean that the wicked will simply be burnt out of existence in the fires of hell, implying that they could not therefore be said to suffer eternally. But this is not the meaning of the text. The intention of the text is not that the wicked will be burnt up but that they will be in the fire eternally (see Mark 9:43–48).

Also, telling against the idea that the wicked are to be completely consumed in hell (and therefore do not have to suffer eternally) is the probability that the last verses of Isaiah would have been understood to provide the background to Jesus' teaching here. In Isaiah 66:22–24 God is promising the new heavens and the new earth which will remain forever before him. He is describing everyone continually coming before him to worship. These people are also said to "go out and look at the dead bodies of the people who have rebelled against me; for their worm shall not die, their fire shall not be quenched . . ." (Isaiah 66:24). For both those worshipping God and those bodies in the unquenchable fire, one of the dominant ideas is its unending nature.

Indeed, the unending nature of suffering in hell portrayed in this verse is not only likely to be part of the background to what Jesus says in Mark 9:43–48; it was also picked up in literature written near the time of the New Testament. One document echoing the Isaiah passage says the wicked "shall weep in pain forever".[8] In short, this passage where Jesus is speaking about the unquenched fire portrays punishment in hell to be never ending.

Another passage in the synoptic gospels that sets out the idea of eternal punishment is Jesus' parable of the talents. That parable concludes with the saying about the slave who hid the master's talent: "As for this worthless slave, throw him into the outer darkness, where there will be weeping and gnashing of teeth" (Matthew 25:30; compare 24:51).[9] While it is true that there is no clear indication of the duration of the suffering, this saying should probably be interpreted in the light of the parable of the sheep and the goats that follows it, the next passage we can note which clearly teaches eternal punishment.

The third passage dealing with eternal punishment in the synoptic gospels is the story of the separation of the sheep and the goats. In that story, the Son of Man is expected to say to some: "You that are accursed, depart from me into the eternal fire prepared for the devil and his angels" (Matthew 25:41). The point is repeated at the end of the story: "And these will go away into eternal punishment, but the righteous into eternal life" (25:46). It is possible that "eternal punishment" means a single punishment that has never-ending consequences. But, as "eternal punishment" and "eternal life" are a balanced pair here, both terms are most probably intended to convey a situation that never ends. Further – and important to our whole discussion – while the word "eternal" can refer to a quality of life in the New Testament it never involves the idea that the life should end. To this we can add an observation on one of the concluding remarks to the parable of the king and the unmerciful servant. Jesus says the unmerciful servant is handed over "to be tortured until he would pay his entire debt" (18:34). What, at first, appears to be an expression of finite punishment turns out to be otherwise, for 10,000 talents (perhaps 150,000 years of a labourer's wages!) could hardly be expected ever to be repaid.

We can only conclude from these three passages, where Jesus is said to be setting out the nature of post-mortem punishment, that it is without end.

*Punishment of uncertain duration*

There is also material in the New Testament that makes it

difficult to hold this view that the wicked are forever punished in hell. This is primarily because, when mention is made of punishment and reward, it comes without giving any obvious indication of its duration. For example, the fourth gospel appears clear on eternal issues. John 3:36 says: "Whoever believes in the Son has eternal life; whoever disobeys the Son will not see life, but God's wrath remains on him" (my translation). John 5:29 says that the time is coming when those in their graves "will come out – those who have done good, to the resurrection of life, and those who have done evil, to the resurrection of condemnation." But there is no indication of how long the condemnation or judgement (*krisis*) is expected to last.

This lack of reference to the length of time of the punishment is also found in Luke 6:23. Jesus is reported as saying, "Rejoice in that day and leap for joy, for surely your reward is great in heaven . . . But woe to you who are rich, for you have received your consolation." From this we cannot tell how long any punishment was thought to last.

Also, in 2 Thessalonians 1:5–10 Paul says that "when the Lord Jesus is revealed" he will be "inflicting vengeance on those who do not know God and on those who do not obey the gospel of our Lord Jesus" (1:8). He then says, "These will suffer the punishment of eternal destruction" (1:9). A first reading of this appears to support the traditional view. However, a more careful reading gives a different result. That is, an examination of the use of the word "destruction" in New Testament times reveals that it could mean either death or annihilation.[10] In any case – and this is important – Paul does not say they will suffer eternal punishment but the punishment of eternal death or destruction.

In short, while there are some passages which are blatantly clear that some people will suffer forever in hell, there are other passages in the New Testament equally clear that we cannot be certain that punishment will be eternal.

So abhorrent do most people find the view that some will forever "burn in hell" that they point out that there is another well-established biblical view.

## 2. Universalism

Universalism is the view that, through God's sheer kindness, everyone will, in the end, be saved. For example, in the United States Hosea Ballou (1771–1852) was the greatest 19th century American Universalist leader. In the early 1800s he persuaded many ministers of the view that, because sin is finite and all its effects are to be experienced in this life, everyone will be saved after death. Also, The Winchester Profession (1803), adopted by the General Convention of Universalists in the New England States at Winchester, New Hampshire, contains the article: "We believe that there is one God, whose nature is Love . . . who will finally restore the whole family of mankind to holiness and happiness."

From what we might hope from a God of love, the majority of us would probably prefer this view. In fact, after fading from interest, during the 20th century universalism came to be accepted across a wide spectrum of Christian traditions, though not generally among all evangelicals.

The most famous early advocate of universalism was Origen. His universalism was based on the view that heavenly creatures who sinned were given earthly bodies as a punishment. However, when they were purified by this punishment they could put away their bodies to rise again to their former state. For a creature to attain perfection, the cycle of discipline in receiving a body and then leaving it behind may have had to be repeated a number of times (*On First Principles* 2:8:3). Origen explains that "through their endurance of greater and more severe punishments of long duration, extending, if I may say so, over many ages . . . they advance through each grade to a higher one, until at length they reach the things that are invisible and eternal" (*On First Principles* 1:6:3).

Due to Origen's dependence on dualism (seeing us as two distinct parts, body and soul) and his reliance upon successive disciplinary reincarnations, he has been vehemently opposed. Few now follow his reasoning. In any case, Origen and his teaching were condemned at two councils of Constantinople (AD 543 and 553), not least because of his view that in the end everyone will be saved. Nevertheless, eschewing speculations characteristic of Origen, and staying more closely to the exegesis of the New Testament, Gregory of Nyssa maintained that God's purpose was "to offer to everyone of us participation in the blessings which are in him" (*On the Soul and the Resurrection*). From the sixth century until the 19th century, Origen's condemnation helped relegate universalism to the position of a minor eccentricity within the church.

## The 20th century

However, Friedrich Schleiermacher (1768–1834), the founding father of liberal Protestantism, and many liberals who followed him – as well as English divines such as Andrew Jukes and the Baptist Samuel Cox – began to argue for universalism. Through the 20th century there was wide and distinguished support for universalism. Nicholas Berdyaev (1874–1948), the Russian mystical philosopher; Anglican Archbishop William Temple (1881–1944); C. H. Dodd (1884–1973), the Congregationalist and premier British New Testament scholar of the 20th century; Charles Raven (1885–1964), the Anglican scholar and vice-chancellor of Cambridge; John Baillie (1886–1960), the Church of Scotland philosopher at New College Edinburgh; Karl Barth (1886–1968), the most prolific and significant theologian of the 20th century; C. F. D. Moule (b. 1908), Lady Margaret's Professor of Divinity in the University of Cambridge from 1951 to 1976 and John A. T. Robinson (1919–1983), the New Testament scholar, dean of Clare College, Cambridge and bishop of Southwark, have all, to varying degrees, advocated universalism. Clearly, universalism cannot be easily dismissed.

For pastoral reasons we might also feel compelled to conclude that everyone will be saved by taking the God whom Christians worship to be a God of love. Not only can we easily imagine that God would want everyone to be saved (see 2 Peter 3:9) but we can also acknowledge that he has the ability to carry out this desire (see John 12:32).

However, as soon as we take into account the generally accepted idea that God has created us with the freedom to choose whether or not we want a relationship with him (now and in any after-life), the idea of universal salvation is less easily maintained. Of course, God could override our freedom and save us all; but that would mean our freedom was a sham. If, as a tract from the 19th century declared, we are all "Doomed to be Saved", then our decisions in relation to God and our enthusiasm for evangelism is considerably undermined.

Nevertheless – to return and follow Origen – this impasse could be overcome by citing 1 Corinthians 13:8 which says that "Love never fails". From this we could conclude that God, in his "love, which is the greatest of all things, will restrain every creature from falling. Then God will be all in all" (compare 1 Corinthians 15:28; Origen, *Romans* 5:10).

In his book *The Great Divorce* (1941) C. S. Lewis said that he could willingly believe that the doors of hell are locked on the inside. Thus, if God is the suffering Father of unending love, we can imagine him as always hammering for admission on hell's locked doors.[11] "If *we* cannot rest without knowing that our loved ones are right with God," asks C. F. D. Moule, "is it conceivable that *God* can be content to let them go?"[12] Perhaps, then, as Bishop John Robinson said, if there was one sinner left in hell, in his love God would return endlessly to encourage the person to repent and accept his love. For God to do otherwise would mark God as a failure or perhaps even as demonic.

## The New Testament and universalism

Unfortunately, the hope of a resolution of the problem as to whether or not all will be saved is not easily fulfilled by turning to the New Testament. But there is a general perspective of the New Testament writers which we can ascertain.

In the writings of Paul, the earliest known Christian writer, we find both views expressed. In Romans 5:18 there is a clear statement concerning universal salvation: "as one man's trespass led to condemnation for all, so one man's act of righteousness leads to justification and life for all." Later in the same letter he says, "For God has imprisoned all in disobedience so that he may be merciful to all" (11:32). Even clearer is 1 Corinthians 15:22: "as all die in Adam, so all will be made alive in Christ." Most famous in this context is the universalist statement of Philippians 2:10–11 that, "at the name of Jesus every knee should bend . . . and every tongue should confess that Jesus Christ is Lord."[13]

To these clear statements from Paul we can add more from other parts of the New Testament. For example, in John's gospel Jesus says, "When I am lifted up from the earth, I will draw all people to myself" (John 12:32, my translation). In the sermon in Acts 3:21 Peter speaks of "the time of universal restoration that God announced long ago through his holy prophets." And as we have already noted, in passing, the writer of 2 Peter 3:9 says that the Lord does not want anyone to perish, but all to come to repentance. There are also other passages which talk about God's activity in Jesus being for the whole world.[14]

However, none of these passages is suggesting that all will be saved, but that ways or means have been provided so that all *could* be saved. Indeed, all of the passages we have just cited come in contexts which refer specifically to the prospect of some people perishing. For example, in 2 Corinthians 5:19 Paul says that "in Christ God was reconciling the world to himself." This is not the basis for any discussion of universalism but the grounds for the possibility of his mission. Similarly, in Colossians 1:20 Paul says that through the Son, "God was pleased to reconcile to himself all things". However, he goes on to say that his readers are now reconciled, provided that they continue steadfast in their faith (1:23). This means that in the passages usually cited to support universalism, the writers cannot have meant to be supporting such a case.

Thus we turn to note that on the other side of the universalism debate there are clear statements that assume that not all will be saved. In Romans Paul says that no one has the power to keep the law and so all are under sin (Romans 3:9). Therefore, says Paul, everyone is under the wrath of God. This means that unbelievers are subject not only to sin and death but also to God's wrath. In 2 Thessalonians 1:8 Paul says that when the Lord Jesus is revealed he will inflict "vengeance on those who do not know God and on those who do not obey the gospel of our Lord Jesus." The assumption here is that there will be others who will escape this ordeal. And, in Romans 9:27 (citing Isaiah 10:22) Paul says "only a remnant of them (the Israelites) will be saved". As we will see, this ambivalence evident in Paul is also reflected in the sayings of Jesus in the gospels.

How do we resolve this apparent conflict of views in the New Testament? Using the New Testament alone it does not seem possible to establish universalism. We could, with John Hick, take the line that while it may be true at any given point on earth that unless we repent we will perish, it could be that, eternally, all will turn from their wickedness and live. On this view, when Jesus was telling people they should repent or be damned he was attempting to change individual behaviour, not formulate theology.[15] But this will not do, for individual statements can be expected to arise out of an overall theology, not to be in conflict with it.

We could speculate that after we have died we get a second chance. But, in the last chapter we argued that such a hope is quite unfounded in the biblical material.

A more promising approach is to argue, as did Bishop John Robinson in his *Honest to God* (1963), that for God's loving purpose to triumph no one can be lost. To do this, God's justice is understood as his correction, leading to a person responding by repenting and attaining final enjoyment of heaven. The problem with this view is that, as we have seen, it does not have the support of the writers of the New Testament. God's wrath is not corrective but retributive.

Another way of supporting universalism would be to argue that the work of Jesus on the cross effectively saved everyone. On this argument, faith or putting one's trust in what has been accomplished is simply acknowledging experientially what one already is in fact. But this understanding is flatly contradicted by the New Testament. The writer of Ephesians puts it quite bluntly that before being incorporated experientially into a relationship with Christ his readers were without hope (Ephesians 2:12–13). The same view is clearly stated in John's gospel where it is said that "everyone who believes in him (the Son Jesus) may not perish but may have eternal life".[16]

In the light of all this, we have to conclude that the case for universalism, while pastorally attractive, does not have the support of the New Testament. In fact, we have seen that the idea of universal salvation is actually countered by the New Testament.

## 3. Conditional immortality

This third traditionally held view of our fate after death is sometimes known as annihilationism. Conditional immortality proposes that our immortality is not inherent but conditional on choices we make in this life: immortality for some, annihilation (rather than eternal suffering punishment) for others. In the early church this idea had a number of proponents. Irenaeus, for example, said that if we keep God's commands we will always remain as we are – immortal; but if we do not keep God's commands we become mortal, melting back into the earth.[17] However, throughout most of the history of Christianity, conditional immortality has not been popular. Indeed, it was condemned at the Fifth Lateran Council in Rome in 1513. Nevertheless, from around the middle of the 19th century, there has been a resurgence of interest in the view, creating considerable disagreement and tension amongst some Christians.

The issue turns around the question as to whether or not the final destiny of those who oppose God is to be endless conscious torment, or total annihilation. Most traditional orthodox, "biblical" or "evangelical" Christians have and continue to hold the view that eternal punishment is the destiny of the so-called lost. Nevertheless, John Stott (b. 1921), who can be taken to speak for others, comments on the traditional position when he says that, "emotionally, I find the concept intolerable and do not understand how people can live with it without either cauterizing their feelings or cracking under the strain."[18]

In surveying the biblical material, John Stott offers four cogent arguments that point in the direction of annihilation. His arguments also make a case that the "eternal conscious torment" view is a tradition which, as he says, has to yield to the supreme authority of Scripture. The four arguments for conditional immortality relate to language, imagery, justice and universalism.

1. *Biblical language.* The language used of the fate of the lost is often that of total destruction. Commonly, various forms of

the words "destruction" (*apōleia*) or "to destroy" or "to kill" (*apollumi*) are used. In Matthew 12:14, for example, the Pharisees conspire how to destroy or kill (*apollumi*) Jesus. Then, showing that hell is a place of destruction or death, Jesus says that the one who can kill or destroy (*apollumi*) both soul and body in hell is to be feared (Matthew 10:28).

If to kill means to destroy life, then to perish in hell is to be eternally extinguished. For example, in John 3:16 eternal life is set over against being killed. God is said to love the world so much that he sent his "only Son so that everyone who believes in him may not perish (*apollumi*) but may have eternal life."[19] And in the Sermon on the Mount Jesus says that "the road is easy that leads to destruction (*apōleia*)" (Matthew 7:13).

The most straightforward implication of this language is that the lost will be annihilated or destroyed on death. The alternative or traditional view of hell as eternal punishment could only make sense of this language by holding a puzzling view that the lost in hell would be in a state of "continual perishing".

A possible reply could be that human beings are, by nature, immortal and indestructible. But, as we have noted a number of times, this is a view borrowed from Greek philosophy. It is not biblical. Where we catch glimpses of the idea of immortality it is only God who naturally has such a characteristic (1 Timothy 1:17; 6:16). For us, immortality is not inherent but a gift from God (2 Timothy 1:10).

2. *Biblical imagery* is a second argument that points in the direction of annihilation rather than perpetual punishment for the lost. Prominent for hell and the fate of the lost is the image of fire. Hell is described as "the fire of hell" (Matthew 5:22; 18:9), "the eternal fire" (18:8; 25:41) and "the lake of fire" (Revelation 20:14–15). This imagery would not have been thought as describing a continuous experience but a

consuming experience. So John the Baptist speaks of Jesus coming to burn the chaff "with unquenchable fire" (Matthew 3:12/Luke 3:17). While the fire is described as eternal and unquenchable, it cannot be imagined that those who enter it would be indestructible, burning eternally. Rather, they would be consumed forever, not tormented forever.

3. *Biblical justice* also favours the idea of annihilation rather than eternal punishment. Fundamental to this idea is that God judges justly and according to what people have done (see Revelation 20:12). This implies that the penalty will be commensurate with the crime. Indeed, it is at the heart of Jewish law depicted in the Bible. For example, in the Jewish courts of the Bible penalties were strictly limited to an exact retribution which is reflected in the famous statement: "you shall give life for life, eye for eye, tooth for tooth, hand for hand, foot for foot, burn for burn, wound for wound, stripe for stripe" (Exodus 21:23–25).

Of course, we would not want to minimize the seriousness of our sin against God. But in the light of the precise justice God sought in the human courts, it is reasonable to ask if it would not be a serious disproportion between sins committed in a limited time, and torment consciously and continually experienced through eternity. Unless we take up the proposal that the lost remain eternally impenitent, perpetual punishment seems incompatible with the biblical view of justice.

4. *Universalism.* The point here is not whether or not everyone will be saved; that we have already discussed earlier in this chapter. Rather, the point is that the forever ongoing existence of the impenitent in hell is difficult to reconcile with the biblical promises of a final victory over evil. For example, in John 12:32 Jesus says: "When I am lifted up from the earth, I will draw all people to myself" (my translation). In 1 Corinthians 15:28 Paul writes of all things being subjected to

Jesus and God being "all in all". Ephesians 1:10 has the idea of all things being gathered up in Christ; and Philippians 2:10 says that every knee shall bow at the name of Jesus.

In the light of what we have said about the unlikely possibility of universalism – all being saved – the most reasonable way to make sense of these statements is to suggest that the only meaningful sense in which God can be said to be "all in all" is that the lost are not left in rebellion to be punished eternally in hell, but are annihilated there.

## Conclusions

To answer the question, "Can a good God condemn some of us to hell?", we must be able to hold together a number of important assertions that arise out of any discussion of this question.

1. God is holy and anyone who is not perfect is unable to be in his presence.
2. Despite the completed and adequate work of Christ making it possible for human beings to be in the presence of a holy God, he has given perfect freedom to his creatures so that they may choose not to be in his presence.
3. God's unconquerable love for all his creation means that he does not want anyone to be outside of the ongoing experience of this love.

To these three core assertions another can be added from earlier discussions in this book.

4. There is nothing in us or about us that makes us naturally immortal; that we live after we die is a gift of God.

The different answers we have seen in this chapter to the problem each reflect the different weights given to these three core assertions. If we hold God's holiness (and concomitant human rebellion) to be the most important assertion, then we may choose to resolve the question by saying that God condemns some people to hell. If we hold God's creation of human freedom to be paramount in this problem, we may also say that God (in response to human freedom) condemns some people to hell. However, if we want to maintain both God's love as well as human freedom, we may solve this puzzle by saying that rather than suffer eternally in hell, some people are annihilated. If, alternatively, we want to hold God's unconquerable love to be the key assertion in this problem, then we find a resolution in either concluding that God allows all his creatures into his presence or that those who do not choose to accept his invitation go out of existence.

We could say no more than that all three of the above core assertions are of equal importance. That would not be helpful, for it would mean the answer to the question, "Can a good God condemn some of us to hell?" would, conveniently, have to remain a mystery to the human mind. Instead, we can take up the perspective of C. S. Lewis and John Robinson. It is what we could call a modified form of universalism, modified in a way that does justice to our free will to choose hell in the face of God's unending love. (The idea of hell is maintained only from our space–time perspective as a way of expressing how people can exist between death and their final submission to the love of God which I suppose to take place at the moment of death.)

So, we can imagine that, if God is the suffering Father of unending love, he is eternally hammering on hell's locked doors for admission. We can also imagine that, if there was one sinner left in hell – any person there who had never had a real opportunity to respond to his love – in his mercy, God would return endlessly to encourage that person to repent and accept his love before experiencing annihilation. In this way we do justice to all three essential assertions: that God is all powerful and holy, that he is a good and loving God, and that he has given his creatures perfect freedom.

## Notes

[1] Augustine, *City of God* 13:2,11, 13: 21:3.

[2] Augustine, *City of God* 20:22; 22.11; compare Minucius Felix, *Octavius* 35:3–4. See also Thomas Aquinas, *Summa Theologica*, Part III, Supplement, Question 94, articles 1 and 3.

[3] Cited by Geoffrey Rowell, *Hell and the Victorians: A Study of the Nineteenth-Century Theological Controversies Concerning Eternal Punishment and the Future Life* (Oxford: Clarendon, 1974), p. 108 and C. S. Rodd, *Is There Life After Death?* (Peterborough, UK: Epworth, 1998), p. 22.

[4] Cited by Fred Carl Kuehner, "Heaven or Hell?" in *Fundamentals of the Faith*, ed., Carl F. H. Henry (Grand Rapids, MI: Baker, 1975), p. 239.

[5] L. L. Morris, "Eternal Punishment", in *Evangelical Dictionary of Theology*, ed., Walter A. Elwell (Grand Rapids, MI: Baker, 1984), p. 370.

[6] For what follows compare Peter M. Head, "The Duration of Divine Judgment in the New Testament", in *"The Reader Must Understand": Eschatology in Bible and Theology*, ed., K. E. Brower and M. W. Elliot (Leicester, UK: Apollos/IVP, 1997), p. 222.

[7] C. S. Lewis, *The Problem of Pain* (London: Bles, 1940), pp. 106–107.

[8] Judith 16:17; compare *1 Enoch* 27:2–3; Isaiah 66:24.

[9] As it is probably a later addition to the gospel, we will leave aside consideration of Matthew 23:14, "Woe to you, scribes and Pharisees, hypocrites! For you devour widows' houses and for the sake of appearance you make long prayers; therefore you will receive the greater condemnation."

[10] 1 Corinthians 5:5; 1 Thessalonians 5:3; 1 Timothy 6:9;

compare *4 Maccabees* 10:15.

[11] Compare David L. Edwards, *After Death?* (London: Cassell, 1999), pp. 154–55.

[12] C. F. D. Moule, *The Meaning of Hope: A Biblical Exposition with Concordance* (London: Highway, 1953), p. 52, his emphasis.

[13] Compare Ephesians 1:10; 1 Timothy 2:4.

[14] 2 Corinthians 5:19; Colossians 1:20; Titus 2:11; Hebrews 2:9; 1 John 2:2.

[15] John Hick, *Death and Eternal Life* (Louisville, KY: Westminster/John Knox, 1994), pp. 248–49.

[16] John 3:16; compare 3:36; Hebrews 10:39.

[17] Irenaeus, *Apostolic Preaching* 15. A view also held by Justin Martyr, Theophilus of Antioch (latter part of the second century), Arnobius (died c. AD 330) and Athanasius ( c. AD 296–373).

[18] In David L. Edwards and John R. W. Stott, *Essentials: A Liberal–Evangelical Dialogue* (London: Hodder & Stoughton, 1990), pp. 314–20 on which I am partly dependent in the next few paragraphs. See also John Wenham, *The Goodness of God* (Leicester, UK: IVP, 1974).

[19] Compare John 10:28; 17:12; Romans 2:12; 2 Peter 3:9.

# 8

## What is Heaven Like?

Most people want to go to heaven, especially to be reunited with friends and relatives. But there is little agreement about what heaven is like. Is it, as the Mormons seem to believe, a "made in America" vision of a busy, family-orientated, hell-bent-for-progress after-life which can be entered if the rules of the church are kept? Perhaps heaven is a garden of indescribable beauty, or even a city with streets paved with gold. Is heaven "up there"? What will we do for ever in heaven? Taking the Bible as our cue, in this chapter we will discover that the reality is far more astounding than is usually thought.

# What is Heaven Like?

"Heaven is for thee too high
To know what passes there; be lowly wise"
John Milton

"Without you, Heaven would be too dull to bear,
And Hell would not be Hell if you were there"
John Sparrow

By and large, heaven is a popular idea. According to a Gallup poll, 77% of Americans believe there is a heaven. 76% think they have a good or excellent chance of getting there.[1] Just what heaven will be like is less clear. In 1983 the popular American religious periodical *U.S. Catholic* reported on readers' beliefs about the after-life. Most of those who responded to the survey described heaven variously as an isolated spot in the country where lots of baseball is played, or as a place filled with whatever pleased each person. Most people thought that heaven would be a peaceful place and many said there would be humour there. A few assumed they would be the same age in heaven as when they die. Even more important than these hopes for heaven was the expectation of being reunited with relatives. People assumed they would meet even their newborn babies who had died but whom they had never seen.

Interestingly, surveys show that the idea of meeting relatives was more important than meeting God, because people do not know what God is like, so it is hard to imagine what it is like to meet him. However, for some, meeting God is of the utmost importance. Bill Prince, a born-again member of a

Southern Baptist church in Atlanta is reported to have said, "The thing about heaven that is most precious to me is the thought of being in the presence of the Saviour and in an environment where everyone there is a believer. Everyone has met the standards of God's entrance requirements, which means that we should all be very much alike."[2]

For others – say a Hindu – heaven is much different. The Hindu heaven is like an extended holiday, a place where our soul rests, perhaps for thousands of years, between our incarnations. Our experience of heaven, from a Hindu perspective, would vary according to the god in residence. But each heaven is expected to be a kind of garden party with flowers, good food, music and beautiful women.

The Mormons have a vividly imagined heaven complete with lakes, forests and cities with lovely, tall buildings. It is, as I noted in the introduction to this chapter, a "made in America" vision of a busy, family-orientated, hell-bent-for-progress after-life which can be entered if the ordinances of the church are kept. Once in heaven there is no time to rest. There is work to be done for the church – converting the dead non-believers and helping "seal" them into the family of the faithful. And the more the individual does in heaven, the greater the progress to ultimate exaltation as gods. However, only the properly married can attain full godhead. For these couples, wives reach their exaltation by taking part in the eternal priesthood of their husband. Eventually, everyone is given glorified bodies to spend forever in painless procreation. The spiritual children take on bodies and inhabit other planets and worship their parents as heavenly father and mother.

This mixture of uncertainty and confidence about beliefs in heaven, which vary from the banal to the bizarre, leaves us wondering what we should believe. If we look at what people have believed in the past about heaven we can see not only the origin of some of these ideas; we can also see what some of our more realistic options are for our hopes about heaven, as well as some ideas that must be discarded.

## Heaven in history

During the Middle Ages, theologians (following Aristotle) took the universe to be a series of concentric spheres. They speculated that hell was the innermost region at the centre of the earth, and it consisted of coarse and unrefined matter. The further one moved out through the spheres, the more luminous and more perfect creation became, until one came to the outer sphere of the firmament which enclosed all things created. Outside this were the two levels of God's realm. Nearest to the created firmament was the "empyrean" (literally "fiery place") or "spiritual heaven" of pure, simple and changeless radiance. This was where God presided over the angels and where the blessed lived. This was their home until after the Last Judgement when it would be their eternal dwelling-place, with their new glorified bodies shining more brightly than the sun. But, God himself – the Trinity – lived above, alone, in the "heaven of heavens", where not even the Blessed Virgin could gain access.

Despite speculations at the time, early in his life Saint Augustine professed a disinterest in attempting any spatial description of eternal life. Nor did he try to locate heaven within the structure of the universe. Instead, thinking such issues to be theologically irrelevant, he encouraged Christians to use their time more profitably than in such speculation.[3] But later in life, Augustine's view of the after-life softened to involve reunions between family members and friends.

Since the Copernican revolution, which dislodged the earth from its illegitimate place at the centre of the universe, and the advent of scientific astronomy which has been able to show us what is "up there", the view of the universe with hell "down there" and heaven "up above" has generally been discarded. As real as they may be (and however they are to be described), the heaven and hell of our after-life are no longer generally seen as part of the universe as we know it. This means we must look for some other account of heaven. If there is anything to be retained from the medieval mind it is that in God's presence there is light and perfection.

## The beatific vision

Thomas Aquinas proposed that the universe was created full of light, but after the sin of Adam and Eve God reduced the luminosity of his creation. However, Aquinas expected that when God renews the universe at the end of time he will increase the luminosity to an intensity beyond its former level, so that the elements will be infused with light and the earth will become semi-transparent and as shiny as glass.

Air will be luminous like a cloudless sky; and water will be like crystal. No longer will heavenly bodies move, for movement implies growth and decay, so that all will stand still like a beautifully polished machine. The world that we know (below the empyrean) will be all but empty: a place to be contemplated, remaining only to function as the dungeon for the damned.[4] While hell is the place of ignorance and obscurity, heaven will be a place of light and especially knowledge, for the highest happiness is to be found in exercising the mind, particularly contemplating and knowing the divine.

Aquinas believed that in heaven we will have a body which God has transformed. In this life our knowledge of God is imperfect because we depend on our imperfect senses. In heaven our senses will not be needed to know God, for we will have immediate and perfect contact with him, bringing perfect love and happiness. No activity will interrupt this tireless, joyful contemplation. The measure of the beatific vision we experience depends on how much we loved God when we were on earth; in heaven no more merit can be gained for, in turn, there is no change in heaven; that would imply that its lower stages were imperfect. Nevertheless, despite a gradation of blessedness, no saint yearns for a greater degree of happiness, for each experiences complete satisfaction and peace in God's will.

According to Aquinas, so completely fulfilled and happy will we be in contemplating God, and so exclusively is he the source of happiness, that not even relating to others will be needed or able to bring us happiness. The only happiness we will find in our relationship with others will be to rejoice in the relationship they also have with God. In part, the downplaying of the importance of the body and human relationships was Aquinas reacting against the Islamic heaven of sexual pleasure.

There is much here that we will need to retain as we piece together a view of heaven that is consistent with the Bible as well as able to withstand the scrutiny of modern minds. The immediate, joyful, tireless and uninterrupted contemplation of God as the essence of heaven must stand as a legitimate hope for Christians, as must the idea that we will have a body. But that there are degrees of life in such an after-life has to be set aside as having little or no basis in the Bible. As we will see towards the end of this chapter, most firmly to be rejected is the idea that earth will, one day, function as the dungeon for the damned.

*Heaven is relationships*

Few have followed Aquinas in his rather Stoic heaven. Bonaventure emphasized love and friendship in heaven, even though those friendships were not expected to be as exclusive as they are on earth. Gertrude of Helfta (1256–1302) used the erotic imagery of the Song of Songs in the Bible to express her heavenly relationship with Jesus, calling him, "O most delicate caresser . . . most ardent lover". She was relying on the guidance of a female German mystic, Mechthild von Magdeburg (c. 1207–82). In her only work, *The Flowering Light of the Godhead*, Mechthild envisioned three heavens.

The lowest or first heaven was an earthly paradise somewhere on earth for those who were neither bad enough to be sent to purgatory nor worthy enough to enter heaven proper. In the second heaven were ten levels of choirs of angels and saints. In the third heaven were the palace and throne of God, as well as the bridal chamber of Christ where an intimate union could take place between Christ and holy women of the highest rank. Besides this beatific union with Christ for the purest of virgins, there was the simple beatific vision near the throne for all the blessed.

There is no doubt that it is legitimate and fitting to envisage our after-life with God or Jesus in the intimate terms provided for us in the Song of Songs. But, once again, we have to set aside not only the idea of purgatory (see chapter 6) but also any idea that there will be any more than one heaven to be enjoyed by all.

## The new Jerusalem

The spread of cities gave writers a new image for describing heaven. Heaven became a city – the new Jerusalem – rather than a garden. The garden or paradise, which was once heaven, became the pleasant surroundings of the celestial city. For example, Gerardesca, a woman who lived as a recluse in Pisa from 1210 to 1269, had visions which we know from an anonymous biography. Reflecting her experience in northern Italy, Gerardesca saw in her visions a vast plain called the territory of the Holy City of Jerusalem. Echoing the longings of the time, everyone was able to experience the good life and live in the warmth, security and nourishment of the heavenly city, rather than live in the oppression of the countryside. The streets of the city-state of the heavenly Jerusalem were paved with gold and precious stones. There was an avenue of golden trees with rich and luxuriant blossom, more beautiful than anything known on earth. The city was surrounded by seven charming castles situated on steep mountains of precious stones. Inside each castle were furnishings of the richest kind and banners of victory depicted the Virgin Mary. In each castle were precious thrones, shining with holy radiance for the Saviour, Mary, the angels, the apostles and prophets, confessors, virgins and all the saints. All were arranged according to rank. Visited three times a year by the entire heavenly court, the castles were filled with incomparable jubilation and glory.[5]

Our response to these visions of the after-life can be brief. As pleasant and comforting as such hopes might be, as we will see later in this chapter, they do not bear up under scrutiny from a biblical perspective. Nevertheless, the visions do capture the beauty and goodness of what God has for his people in the after-life.

## Dante's journey

In the long narrative poem *The Divine Comedy* by Dante, we catch a glimpse of the hopes of heaven imagined by someone in the Middle Ages. In what may be the greatest piece of literature ever written, Dante describes in three sections – *Inferno, Purgatorio* and *Paradiso* – his spiritual journey from darkness and error to the revelation of the divine light, culminating in the beatific vision of God.

Down through the descending circles of the pit of hell Dante is guided by the ancient Roman poet Virgil, who represents the epitome of human knowledge. Passing Lucifer at the pit's bottom – at the dead-centre of the earth – Dante and Virgil emerge on the beach of the island mountain of Purgatory (see chapter 6). At the summit of Purgatory, where repentant sinners are purged of their sins, Virgil departs, having led Dante to the limits of human knowledge, the threshold of Paradise. There Dante is met by Beatrice, who embodies the knowledge of divine mysteries given by God. She leads him through the successive ascending levels of heaven to the empyrean, where she takes her leave of Dante. Beatrice joins the blessed who are seated in a vast rose-shaped amphitheatre below the Trinity and the angels. Dante is able to see the nine orders of angels in the form of circles of light spinning around the brilliant point of God's light at the centre. After smiling briefly at Dante, Beatrice returns her gaze to God. Utterly alone, Dante is then left to stand before God, absorbed into the glorious light of God.

> Within its depthless clarity of substance
> I saw the Great Light shine into three circles.[6]

In this triumvirate of light Dante perceives the features of a man – Christ. Dante also senses an impulse of love so immense that it moves the sun and the other stars. Dante has arrived at his destination, and the poem ends with the merging of his love with that of the divine for "there is nothing to be sought beyond."

## The Renaissance and Reformation

The pleasures Aquinas denied and the mystics sought in heaven were developed and described more fully in the Renaissance period with its revival of classical learning.[7] For example, through his *On Old Age* and *Scipio's Dream*, Cicero (105–43 BC), the Roman orator and statesman, provided the Florentine poet Petrarch (1304–74) with resources for speculating that, on dying, old friends would meet in heaven. The poet Tibullus (55–19 BC) inspired the Dominican Francesco Colonna (1433–1527) to describe the dying as entering a world of fountains and fields with nymphs and their lovers. Imbibed with images of the time, the Christian humanist and most important European scholar of his time, Desiderius Erasmus (1466–1536) of Rotterdam imagined that on dying we would be greeted by a saint who would give our naked bodies a beautiful robe. Having been embraced and guided to an elevated place in this paradise, heaven would open for us to ascend into the presence of God.

Leaders of the Reformation in the 16th century reacted against this human-orientated thinking. They replaced the after-life with a God-centred hope. At the funeral of his friend Martin Luther, Philipp Melanchthon (1497–1560) said in his Latin oration, "Let us rejoice that he now holds that familiar and delightful conversation with God, His son, our Lord Jesus Christ." Melanchthon expected Luther to have "entered that vastly higher school, where he can contemplate the essence of God" and see the Saviour "face to face", rejoicing with unspeakable joy, pouring forth thanks to God for his great goodness. This was a hope Luther had expected all to be able to enjoy, for we would all be equal in heaven. There were no hierarchies in heaven.

Reminiscent of those before him, Luther described heaven to his little son as "a pretty, beautiful garden where there are many children wearing little golden coats. They pick up fine apples, pears, cherries, and yellow and blue plums under the trees. They sing, jump, and are merry. They also have nice ponies." Luther described heaven as a place where we would have glorified bodies constantly sustained by God. Like Aquinas, he also reacted against the Islamic idea, saying that only heathen fools would want bodies that produced urine and faeces. Despite what he said to his son about fruit-picking, Luther imagined that our glorified bodes would not need food and that we would float through space with the sun and other creatures as our playthings. Luther did not think that earth would be eliminated but would be a delight to behold.

Calvin also thought the earth would be renewed. His evidence was the statement in Matthew 5:5: "Blessed are the meek, for they will inherit the earth." Calvin, as well as Luther, thought that perfected plants and animals would remain on the new earth forever. However, the new earth was not the place for us for all eternity. Luther thought that we could visit the earth. Calvin thought that we would not even be interested in the new earth, which had been re-created simply as part of God's vision until the final judgement, when the earth would be no more.

As far as our life together is concerned, Luther considered that we would still retain our gender, but all other distinctions between us such as profession, wealth and laws would be gone. With God as the only ruler we will all be equal. Calvin even thought that, since marriage implied submission, married couples would be torn apart from each other. Similarly, depending on the widespread influence of Cicero's views, Luther thought that we would meet our dead relatives in heaven but we would not relate to them as relatives. Calvin showed no sentimentality. He thought that living in heaven was to have God as the focus of attention and enjoyment and that we would not be talking to or listening to each other.

## The Counter-reformation and English divines

For Roman Catholics after the Counter-reformation, the newly established heliocentric nature of the universe was brought into service as a model for the spiritual universe. Hence, in paintings the heavenly court is depicted as encircling God as planets encircle the sun. In our future life our eternal joy is expected to consist of focusing on God and enjoying his perfect beauty and glorious goodness (see *Catechism of the Council of Trent*, 1566). Frequently appearing in art, presiding over all the other saints, is Mary, the Queen of the Angels or the Empress of Heaven. Sometimes she is sitting near Christ the judge, softening his sentences.

Some Catholics included a renewed earth as part of their vision of the future. For example, it was speculated that after the Last Judgement the earth would be cleansed and glorified, and even if not good enough for the blessed, it could provide a place for unbaptized children to live.

The principal concern of the English Puritan divine, Richard Baxter (1615–91), was to portray the after-life as comprising our enjoyment of God; any other joys would stem from this. Like many others at the time, one of the joys Baxter promoted was the singing of everlasting praise in heaven. However, while a joy, singing only existed for the worship of God. Congregational singing was the necessary preparation for this. He put it bluntly: "A swine is fitter for a lecture of philosophy or an ass to build a city . . . than you are for this work of heavenly praise."[8] Once again we find the expectation that we will meet others in the after-life, Baxter even listing 44 people such as Luther and Calvin whom we could expect to see among all the saints of all ages who will be there. In line with the Puritan's love of learning, so perfect is heaven that we will, according to Baxter, know in an instant all that is to be known.

## A turning point

It is probably to a Swedish mystic and scientist, Emanuel Swedenborg (1688–1772), that we owe the view of heaven that is most commonly held by Christians today. Pursuing the life of a scientist, mathematician and engineer, the wealthy Swedenborg read and travelled extensively in England and wrote on a wide variety of subjects. He was heavily influenced by John Locke, Isaac Newton and Henry More. Refusing a professorship in mathematics at Uppsala, he became a member of the Swedish board of mines. In 1744 and 1745 his journal records dreams of a spiritual crisis. Two years later, at the age of 59, he retired to turn his attention from his astute observations of the natural world to his visions of something indescribable that had thrown him to the ground and forced him to pray. By the time of his death he had produced about three dozen volumes of writings based on his visions.[9]

Immanuel Kant, a contemporary of Swedenborg, saw his books as full of nonsense.[10] Nevertheless, Swedenborg provided a view of heaven which, rather than being God-centred, is focused on a number of characteristics that are satisfyingly human in orientation.

First, he considered that there was only a thin veil which divides heaven and earth. The purgatory of the Catholics and the sleeping of the souls after death until the Last Judgement maintained by Luther and Calvin are denied or minimized. The righteous enter heaven immediately after death.

Secondly, Swedenborg's heaven is not structurally opposite to life on earth. Even though it may have once been seen as a frivolous pastime, an important aspect of life in heaven will be a continuation and fulfilment of our present life with its material and sensual qualities.

Thirdly, gone are the ideas of a static heaven. Eternal rest has saints engaged in activities and experiencing change and spiritual progress. All this joyful activity takes place in an environment that is dynamic and full of motion. This is because reaching heaven is not the end of spiritual development but part of the eternal journey towards God. People are not punished or purged in this journey. Rather, in association with others of a similar level of spiritual development, angels guide and encourage people to shift attention from the external loveliness of heaven to more important inner concerns until they are ready for the higher state of heaven, when they become angels.

Fourthly, no longer is heaven understood primarily as the experience of divine love through the beatific vision. Instead, God's love is experienced not only directly, but also through the love shown in social relations, especially the marriage love between men and women which is the foundation of all other love. However, a husband and wife may not continue as a married couple in heaven if one of them is not of the same spiritual development. Instead, couples might split and find more compatible partners and be married in heaven, even enjoying "blessed intercourse". The offspring of these unions are love and wisdom, rather than babies.[11]

Thus, Swedenborg's visions marked a turning point in the view of heaven. No longer was heaven a static state. It was a place of growth and progress. What was once primarily a beatific vision of the divine was now a heaven where the cultivation of human love was the main purpose of heaven. Heaven was no longer a new and transformed earth, but became earth purged of the ugly and unnecessary. God's love could then be experienced through the key relationships of society, love, marriage, children, family and friends. There had been a shift in heaven from *eternal* life to eternal *life*.

## Today . . .

The popular view of heaven has changed little from what Swedenborg envisaged. The Gallup poll mentioned at the start of this chapter reported that 91% of the respondents thought that heaven would be peaceful; 83% thought they would be with God; 77% that they will see people they know. Interestingly, 74% expect there to be humour in heaven.

However, the expectations of the after-life set out by theologians is often vastly different from popular belief. By the middle of the 20th century some theologians had all but dispensed with heaven, as did Hans Jonas (1903–93), ironically, in his "Ingersoll Lecture on the Immortality of Man" delivered before a large crowd in Andover Chapel, Harvard Divinity School, in 1961. He declared that we will have no individual, conscious after-life. Instead, all we can hope for is to be eternally remembered by God or, mythically speaking, to be inscribed into the heavenly Book of Life.

In our own time, theologians are generally not as pessimistic; however, they still offer few details about our after-life. For example, David Edwards, retired provost of Southwark Cathedral and sub-dean of Westminster Abbey, as well as Speaker's chaplain in the House of Commons, has a minimalistic view of heaven. He says that, "When we die we go not to the stars, not to Summerland, not to fairyland and not to any 'other world', but to God, without end." He does not expect that after death life will be an unchanging immortality of our soul. That would bring boredom. He does not think our present body will be reassembled with improvements, for that would mean the total reversal of the laws of creation. Nor will we be absorbed into God. That would not allow what is valued in us continuing beyond death. Rather, Edwards speculates, "We shall be embraced – embraced by What and Who is reality more real than anything or anyone known by us previously." He goes on to say that if we are prepared to be embraced, in the change made within us when time is replaced by eternity and when space is replaced by the glory of God, we will experience our liberating cleansing or purgatory preparing us for final glory. Quoting Augustine, he then sums up his expectations of heaven: "There we shall rest and see, we shall see and love, we shall love and praise."[12]

## Heaven and the Bible

For those who want to think clearly about life after death in the light of the Bible, and develop their thinking along a biblical trajectory, it is important that we examine what the Bible has to say about heaven. This might enable us to choose between or perhaps modify and take up some of the views we have seen emerge from our survey of the history of heaven. We may even need to discard entirely popular views of the after-life.

When we were examining life after death in the Old Testament we saw that writers seem to have been hesitant to speculate about life after death to the point that, at one stage of the history of the people of God, death was seen as the end. What hints of immortality and particularly resurrection there are in the Old Testament remain enigmatic at best.

Most of the references to heaven are found in the New Testament, so we shall focus our attention there. As we gather sample references we need to be cautious, for we would be put off the scent of our search for heaven if we simply looked for the word "heaven". We will see that New Testament writers use the word differently from what we expect. And what the New Testament has to say about what we call heaven is not limited to the occurrence of the word.

## Clearing the ground

There are some references in the New Testament which do not help us, for they simply refer to the sky: for example, where Jesus speaks of heaven as the realm of birds (Matthew 6:26) and clouds (Mark 14:62).

Surprisingly for some, we also need to set aside the phrase "the kingdom of heaven" as a description of life after death. Matthew has the word "heaven" 32 times in the phrase "kingdom of heaven" – which is not used anywhere else in the New Testament. For example, at one point Jesus is reported as saying that, "unless your righteousness exceeds that of the scribes and Pharisees, you will never enter the kingdom of heaven" (Matthew 5:20). If we were not alert to the meaning of the phrase in Matthew's gospel we could take this to refer to how we can enter life after death. However, in line with his Jewish sensitivities about using the name of God, the phrase is Matthew's substitute for Mark and Luke's "the kingdom of God", which simply means the reign or authority of God. In short, the phrase "the kingdom of heaven" is not a description of the future life after death; it refers to God's reign or rule begun in the ministry of Jesus which, however, can be expected to continue after death.

## Making progress

To begin assembling our picture of heaven we can note that, in the teaching of Jesus, heaven is the realm of God (Matthew 5:16), of Jesus (John 6:38), and of the Spirit (15:26), as well as of the angels (Mark 13:32). It is also the place to which Jesus is said to have ascended (Luke 24:51), and from where he will one day return (Acts 1:11).

With care, we gain some understanding of the nature of heaven and our anticipated experience of it in the phrase "eternal life", well known from John's gospel but also found a few times in the other gospels. The term appears 17 times in John and six times in 1 John. Even without the qualification of "eternal", the word "life" in the Johannine writings does not refer to this earthly or natural life. Instead, life or eternal life is a gift from God through the Spirit in Jesus.[13] The most fundamental aspect of eternal life is that it is the life that God has in himself (John 5:26); Jesus comes from this life and also has this life (6:57). Also essential in advancing our thinking about heaven and eternal life is the idea that Jesus was sent to give eternal life to people still living in this earthly life (1:4). Importantly, this (eternal) life is not extinguished nor is it interrupted by death (11:26) but continues beyond it. Indeed, in Matthew 7:14 Jesus says that "life" is to be the experience after death (compare Mark 9:43–48). This means we can define eternal life as the life of God which we can expect to experience in the after-life but which Jesus already gives in this life to those who believe in him. In other words, heaven can be anticipated as a continuation of the experience of God's life which we have before death.

The term "eternal life" is also found, though less often, in the Pauline letters. Nevertheless, our conclusions are fully supported by Paul's use of the term. For example, Paul says that his readers have already been freed from sin to experience eternal life (Romans 6:22–23). And in Galatians 6:8–9 eternal life is clearly expected to continue in the after-life, for in Paul's mind eternal life is the opposite to decay and corruption (compare John 3:16).

This glimpse into the meaning of "eternal life" in John and Paul informs us that our experience of the after-life – heaven – will, in some way, be a continuation of our experience of God on earth through knowing him and Jesus (John 17:3).

## Mark 13

This passage, often called "the little apocalypse", can also be brought into service in trying to build a biblical understanding of heaven. The majority of scholars see woven together here Jesus' teaching both on the fall of Jerusalem as well as the end of the world, though just which of Jesus' sayings refer to which event is the source of considerable debate. Nevertheless, there is less uncertainty about verses 24–26 referring to "the End":

> the sun will be darkened,
> and the moon will not give its light,
> and the stars will be falling from heaven,
> and the powers in the heavens will be shaken.
> Then you will see "the Son of Man coming in clouds" with great power and glory. Then he will send out the angels, and gather his elect from the four winds, from the ends of the earth to the ends of heaven.

The cosmic dimension of this passage suggests that we are dealing with an understanding of the end of the world as we know it. But the interpretation of such apocalyptic language, similar to that found in Isaiah 13 and 34 and Daniel 7:13–14, is notoriously hazardous. So much depends on what meaning is given to the various images. Nevertheless, even without a detailed examination, the import of this passage is clearly that the coming of the Son of Man – the glorified Jesus Christ – to gather up those who belong to him at "the End" of time will involve the cosmic collapse of all that we know. Thus, whatever else happens after the end of this life, it will not involve a simple continuation of life on earth. Before making use of this conclusion there are some other New Testament passages to take into account in understanding heaven.

## Other passages

In Mark 12 some Sadducees (who said there was no resurrection of the dead) come to Jesus in order to ridicule him about his beliefs on the after-life (see Luke 14:14). The Sadducees spin an unlikely story about a woman whose seven successive husbands die, all of them brothers. Their question is, "In the resurrection whose wife will she be?" (Mark 12:23). To begin with, Jesus replies, in effect, by saying that the basis of their ridicule of his belief in the resurrection of the dead is due to their not knowing the power of God, by which he presumably means, power to raise the dead (see 1 Corinthians 6:14). Then Jesus says that those raised from the dead do not marry (Mark 12:25). At first this seems to imply that the after-life is relationally cold and sterile. More likely, Jesus is proposing both that the depths of relations in the after-life will transcend those experienced on earth and that such satisfaction will come from being in the glory of God's presence (compare Babylonian Talmud *Berakoth* 17a). Thus human relationships will not need to have their present significance. This may be what Jesus means when he says that in the resurrection people will be like angels (Mark 12:25); human relationships will find their fulfilment in the brother–sister relationships of a community (see *The Community Rule* [1QS] 11:7–8).

Galatians 4.26 provides an interesting perspective on heaven in speaking of Sarah corresponding "to the Jerusalem above". But again this is not testimony to our need to ascend to another place to experience heaven. Paul has in mind Jewish apocalyptic thinking which presumed there was an ideal form of Jerusalem in heaven to which we would not have to ascend but which would be revealed here on earth (compare *2 Baruch* 4:2–6; *4 Ezra* 7:26). Indeed, making use of the same imagery, Hebrews 12.22 talks of the heavenly Jerusalem not as something future or in another place, but as being part of present experience.

In Philippians 3:20 Paul says that "our citizenship is in heaven". This could be taken to mean that our life after death – be it understood as entered into at our individual death before "the End", or taking place in "the End" – involves leaving this earth of time and space to go to another place without time or space. However, Paul does not say that our experience of life after death – the transformation of our bodies – will take place when we leave earth and go to heaven. Instead, he says here that he expects Jesus to come from heaven to earth in order to transform us. Again we need to keep this in mind when we assemble a picture of what we can expect heaven to be.

The writer of 1 Peter 1:4 says that God has given us an inheritance that is "kept in heaven for you". On a first reading this could be taken to mean that in order to experience our post-mortem inheritance we need to leave this earth to obtain it in heaven. But this cannot be the intention of the writer. Instead, in line with current expectations (*1 Enoch* 48:7; 58:5; *Ascension of Isaiah* 8:25–26), he means that our inheritance, which is secured and protected in heaven, is already being dispensed to us. He says that his readers are already experiencing what is secured in heaven (1 Peter 1:5–9; compare Colossians 1:5).

Importantly, when we turn to the book of Revelation we get a very clear description of heaven not as a futuristic, geographically separate place from earth. Rather the writer says that, for those with patient endurance, the new Jerusalem comes down out of heaven (Revelation 3.12; compare 21:2, 10). Heaven is a present experience for those who live by faith in Jesus, not counting the cost as they bear witness to him.

*What is heaven like?*

The place and picture of heaven that is emerging from the New Testament writings is very different from the celestial

city above the earth that we encounter in popular thinking or
that has come down to us in the history of thinking about
heaven. We must discard the old idea either that heaven has
various parts or that access is denied to some. Also, the idea
that God is alone in heaven may safeguard his holiness, but it
does violence to the biblical view that in the after-life God
and his people will be together.

The enormous difference between what we see in the Bible
and almost all the images with which we are familiar is that
heaven will be the enveloping of life on earth by the life of
God and his heavenly court. We will not go up to heaven. In
the cosmic and complete collapse and creative renewal of
earth in the ending of time, heaven will have come to earth.
Either at our individual death or in "the End", heaven will be
experienced as a continuation of what we have begun to experience as a foretaste.

In order to hold in tension the two ideas that, on the one
hand, our individual death is the portal to our after-life in
heaven and, on the other hand, that heaven will involve the re-
creating transformation of this earth, we can keep in mind the
idea found in Paul that after death we will sleep until "the
End". But we have seen that this sleep is neither real nor
apparent to the individual who dies before "the End"; it is
only apparent to those remaining alive on earth. Thus, in the
moment of our death we will experience the full after-life God
has for us: life on a re-created earth renewed by God having
transformed it by his powerful presence.

There is little more detail that we are able to deduce from
the Bible. The idea that heaven will be boring arises from the
idea that it is only in ceaseless activity that we find purpose in
life. There is no reason why that need be the case. We know
from the teaching of Jesus that there will be no marriage in
heaven (Mark 12:25). Our being in the presence of and enjoying the company of God as well as the depth of relationship
with each other will be so significant as to eclipse the need

and desire for marriage. Thus not only will we know each other intimately; we will be in the presence of God the Father, Son and Holy Spirit – enjoying the immediate, joyful, tireless and uninterrupted worship and contemplation of him. The final book of the Bible, the Revelation of Saint John, attempts to depict being in God's company. Even without knowing the precise meaning of all the images, we can appreciate the power and joy of heaven captured in this passage from chapter 4.

> I looked, and there in heaven a door stood open! . . . I was in the spirit, and there in heaven stood a throne, with one seated on the throne! And the one seated there looks like jasper and carnelian, and around the throne is a rainbow that looks like an emerald . . . Coming from the throne are flashes of lightning, and rumblings and peals of thunder . . . Around the throne, and on each side of the throne, are four living creatures . . . Day and night without ceasing they sing,
>> "Holy, holy, holy,
>> the Lord God Almighty,
>>> who was and is and is to come."

## Notes

[1] Reported by Kenneth L. Woodward, "Heaven: This is the Season to Search for New Meaning in Old Places", *Newsweek/Bulletin,* (Sydney, 4 April 1989), p. 69.

[2] Kenneth L. Woodward, "Heaven: This is the Season to Search for New Meaning in Old Places", *Newsweek/Bulletin,* (Sydney, 4 April 1989), pp. 69–70.

[3] Augustine, *Genesis* 2:9–10. Compare Lactantius, *Divine Institutes* 3:3.

[4] Aquinas, *Summa Theologica*, Suppl. 91:3, 4; 97:4.

[5] Giacomino of Verona, "The Heavenly Jerusalem", 61–68 in Esther I. May, *The De Jerusalem celesti and the De Babylonia infernali of Fra Giacomino da Verona* (Florence: Le Monnier,

1930), p. 75, translated from Joseph Tusiani, *The Age of Dante* (New York: Baroque, 1974), 137. Cited in Colleen McDannell and Bernhard Lang, *Heaven: A History* (New Haven and London: Yale University Press, 1988), p. 76 and note 9 on p. 367.

[6] Dante, *Paradise* 33:115–117.

[7] On what follows see Colleen McDannell and Bernhard Lang, *Heaven: A History* (New Haven and London: Yale University Press, 1988), chapters 5 and 6.

[8] Richard Baxter, *The Saints' Everlasting Rest* (London: Underhill & Tyton, 1649), p. 273 cited by Colleen McDannell and Bernhard Lang, *Heaven: A History* (New Haven and London: Yale University Press, 1988), p.174.

[9] See, for example, Emanuel Swedenborg, *Heaven and its Wonders* and *Hell: From Things Heard and Seen* (London: The Swedenborg Society, 1958).

[10] Immanuel Kant, *Dreams of a Spirit-Seer Illustrated by Dreams of Metaphysics* (1766). See Ernst Cassirer, *Kant's Life and Thought* (New Haven and London: Yale University Press, 1981), pp. 77–92.

[11] From Colleen McDannell and Bernhard Lang, *Heaven: A History* (New Haven and London: Yale University Press, 1988), chapter 7.

[12] David L. Edwards, *After Death? Past Beliefs and Real Possibilities* (London: Cassell, 1999), p. 160, compare 158–60.

[13] Compare John 3:16; 5:24; 6:63; 20:22, 31.

# 9

## How Can We Live if We are Going to Die?

If life after death is one of the "probable certainties" of life, we need to prepare to die. But how do we prepare to die? How can we prepare to live after death rather than be annihilated? And if death is not our end, if we continue to live after death, we must face another issue. As Ernest Hemingway put it, "How can we live, seeing we have to die?"

# How Can We Live if We are Going to Die?

"Who knows whether to live is to be dead,
or to be dead is to live"
Socrates

"It matters not how a man dies but how he lives.
The act of dying is not of importance,
it lasts so short a time"
Samuel Johnson

Once upon a time, before we became disillusioned in this postmodern world, there seemed to be hope. There was the hope that our families would be safe and secure places; there was the hope that we were solving the environmental issues; there was the hope that we were learning how to live peaceably with each other; and there was the hope that our world was becoming a better and safer place for us and our children.

A 20th century of war, environmental mismanagement and disasters has eroded our hopes for a better future. More and more of us are living in despair. No longer is John Lennon's 1971 song "Imagine" only imagination: for most people, there is no heaven – or hell – and the majority of us are living for today.

A 19-year-old man stood on a ledge 17 storeys above Fifth Avenue in New York. Police and firemen sought to get him to come down, but he shouted to those near him, "I am a lonely man. I wish someone could convince me life is worth living." And he jumped.

If there was hope for the future – if there was a wider perspective on life than what we are able to grasp during these mortal years – we would truly be able to live. The best known of all German poets, Johann Goethe (1749–1832) speaks for us when he says: "if only the eternal remains present to us at every moment, then we do not suffer from the transience of time."

Throughout the chapters of this book, we have been trying to distill from the Bible, as well as from clear thinking and the vagaries of life, what we might be certain about regarding our future. At the beginning of chapter five I drew attention to the fear of death that many people share. But not everyone fears the grave. In the final pages of his last book, *Conversion* (1988), Malcolm Muggeridge (1903–1990), the British journalist and media figure, wrote frankly of his looming death: "So, like a prisoner awaiting his release, like a schoolboy when the end of term is near, like a migrant bird ready to fly south, like a patient in hospital anxiously scanning the doctor's face to see whether a discharge may be expected, I long to be gone."

I had not thought a great deal about death in my youth. But, having had a near-death experience or close encounter with death (see chapter 1), one of the strong impressions I was left with was that there was nothing to be feared in death. Dr E. Kübler-Ross has found a similar conclusion: "Not one of the patients who's had this experience was ever again afraid to die. Not one of them, on all our cases."[1] But we face a problem in being certain about life after death.


## Certainties?

Except for Jesus, no one has ever been there and returned to tell us about life after death. (Lazarus and others who were raised to die again returned to this life. In contrast we could say that Jesus went right through death to be raised beyond this life, even though he could still participate fully in this life.) Yet, through this study, we have discovered that, as uncertain as the future may be, there are "probable certainties" in the uncharted waters beyond the grave:

● Death is not the end. While there may be nothing inherently immortal about us as individuals, we can only make logical and moral sense of our life-experience on this planet if we live beyond the grave. Reports of near-death experiences may be hints of our life after death, made possible by God. From our survey of ancient cultures, it appears that the expectation that we will live again is woven into the very fabric of our human psyche. The reluctance of God's people during most of the Old Testament times to speculate about life after death could have been due to their concern that people living beyond the grave might compromise their monotheism.

● There is nothing intrinsically impossible about reincarnation. However, there are strong reasons to set aside this idea if we are going to think clearly about life after death: reincarnation does not allow us to continue to live as conscious individuals in a next life; reincarnation foists past evil on innocent victims who are destined to perpetuate and multiply the tragic weight of the past; reincarnation is not proved by past-life recall, which is to be accounted for by such factors as mediumship, seances, spirit contact, demon possession, psychic trance utterances or cryptoamnesia; and reincarnation is specifically condemned by the Bible and the early church.

● Do we have an immortal soul? Yes and no! We do have a soul, but our soul has no independent existence enabling it to live on beyond the grave without our body. From an examination of the Bible, as well as Christian and secular thinking (both ancient and modern), we can expect to experience life after death as an integrated person.

● The event of the bodily resurrection of Jesus turns the conjecture into a conviction that our present bodies will be involved in our life after death. By a miraculous new action of creation God will provide us with a resurrected and transformed spirit-orientated body.

- It will appear to us that we will receive our new bodies immediately we die. For those of us who are left alive in the dimension of this space-time it will appear that the dead are waiting for us to join them so that we will all receive our transformed bodies at "the End" of time.

- The ideas of purgatory and limbo are to be discarded as an insult to the care of a loving God. These ideas also mock the power of God to make us fit – in an instant – to live with him. Further, these ideas are an affront to the suffi- ciency of the preparatory work of Christ. If there is no purgatory nor limbo, praying for the dead is only a com- fort for those who remain in this life.

- There is a hell for those who are not perfect! It will proba- bly be the hell of annihilation. Yet, paradoxically, as God is unconquerably and eternally loving, he will forever be hammering on the doors of hell, endlessly encouraging those within to repent and accept his love and provision for life with him.

- Heaven will not be the celestial city of modern sentimen- tality. At the moment of our death – coincidental with "the End" for those who remain alive – heaven will be the envelopment of our life on earth by the life of God and his heavenly court. In a cosmic and complete re-creative mir- acle that will renew the whole of creation, heaven will have "come down" to earth to continue the life we have already begun to experience here with God.

- If there is nothing intrinsically immortal about us, and only the perfect are able to experience life after death, entry into life after death is a gift from God.

There may be no absolute certainties about life after death. But there are more than enough hints in our present experience and from the Bible to be sure of the possibility of living beyond the grave, providing we have a relationship with God this side of death. This raises the question as to how we should prepare to die.

## Preparing to die

An 18th century epitaph says it all:

> Remember, friends, as you pass by,
> As you are now, so once was I.
> As I am now, so you must be
> Prepare yourself to follow me.

Writing in *The Spectator* (London, 31 July 1999), Peter Chadlington reminds us that at the end of our youth there is a moment we face: we stop looking forward to an endless future. Instead we start counting the time we have left: only so much time to get it all done, to gather it all and fit it all in. Then, a little later, we begin to contemplate the manner of our end.

Chadlington notes that the upsurge of interest in death is reflected by some eight weeks in which a little book, *Conversations with Morrie*, was at or near the top spot on the US non-fiction best-seller lists. This book recounts the conversations between a former student, now middle-aged, and his dying university professor, and the lessons he has learned of life and, particularly, of death.

Over 80% of adults want to die quickly and happily, according to a recent survey in the United States. Most of us want to die quickly and painlessly.

But such sudden, unannounced ends leave us no time for preparation for the one certain irreversible event. Studies done of people facing death reveal that what concerns them is not the pain – that can generally be managed by modern medicine – but the search for inner peace. In *How we Die: Reflections of Life's Final Chapter* (New York: Random, 1994) Sherwin B. Nuland tells us that not only do people search for peace in the face of death, but that all the baggage of life – personal pride, long-held resentments – build up to provide an insurmountable hurdle in our last days.

We are urged by so many that we ought not wait until we are on our deathbed to set about preparing for death: righting wrongs and relationships. Chadlington is right that deathbed conversions are rare; not many of us relinquish a lifetime of beliefs in the closing moments of life. We must prepare for death ASAP – as soon as possible. Even if God does not exist and the whole religious edifice of the East as well as the West is a hoax or a fabric of our imagination, there is still inherent value in the kindness, justice, mercy and reconciliation that result from preparing to die.

Indeed, asserts Chadlington, regardless of the relevance of religion, we die best when we prepare earliest. Socrates urged that we "always be occupied in the practice of dying". Even at the age of 58 the Dalai Lama said it was time for him to prepare for death.

*How do we prepare to die?*

If we have no expectation of life after death we may seek immortality in this life. Some people are now seeking immortality in this world through having themselves written into novels. I do not know Shelaine Green's attitude to life after death. Nevertheless, towards the end of the year 2000, *The Observer* (London, 10 December) reported that Shelaine has paid over £6,000 to have her name used as a character in the next novel by Kathy Lette. However, if we are concerned about whether or not we – we as an individual person, not just our name – live on after we die, we need to know how to prepare to die. An interesting story illustrates that our preparation needs to be more profound than we might think.

## The price of entry

Franz-Josef I of Austria was the last emperor of the Hapsburg empire, which had its origins in the thirteenth century. Franz-Josef died on 21 November 1916, during the First World War. A few days later, at the funeral on 30 November, the splendid pageantry of one of the greatest empires Europe had ever known was displayed for the last time. Eight black horses drew the hearse containing the coffin, which was draped in the black and gold imperial colours. The hearse was preceded by carriages filled with wreaths. In turn, these carriages were preceded by barouches seating the highest court dignitaries. Behind this procession came the carriages carrying the members of the family and the foreign officials. Mounted guards in their dress uniform escorted the procession along the Ringstrasse, across Vienna, to St. Stephen's Cathedral. A band played sombre music.

After the service the cortège covered the few hundred metres to the Capuchin crypt on foot. By the light of flaming torches, the cortège descended the steps of the crypt. At the bottom was a great iron door leading to the Hapsburg family crypt. Behind the door was the abbot. With the Grand Master of the court he began the ritual dialogue, established centuries before.

The Grand Master, Prince Montenuovo, cried out, "Open!" The abbot responded, "Who are you? Who asks to enter here?" The Grand Master began to list the emperor's 37 titles: "We bear the remains of his Imperial and Apostolic Majesty, Franz-Josef I, by the grace of God Emperor of Austria, King of Hungary, Defender of the Faith, Prince of Bohemia-Moravia, Grand Duke of Lombardy, Venezia, Styrgia . . ." And so he continued through the whole 37 titles. However, the abbot called back, "We know him not. Who goes there?" The Prince spoke again. This time he used a much abbreviated and less ostentatious title reserved for times of expediency. But, again, the abbot responded, "We know him not. Who goes there?"

The Grand Master tried a third time. He stripped the emperor of all but the humblest of titles. Going down on his knees, he simply cried out, "We bear the body of Franz-Josef, our brother, a sinner like us all."

At that the door swung open and the abbot said, "Enter then." And Franz-Josef was admitted.

This story illustrates the biblical perspective that our entry into life after death depends not on what we have achieved (or not achieved) in this life, but on knowing we do not deserve what can only be a gift to us.

We avoid being lost forever after death, and we receive the gift of life after death – life in the presence of God – by beginning life with God now, so that when we die we are able to continue to be with God. This is a theme woven through the gospel of John.

There have been many suggestions as to how we begin a relationship with God. I suggest that we keep in mind passages in the Bible such as Ephesians 2:8–9: "by God's love you have been saved through trusting him, and this is not your own doing; it is the gift of God" (my paraphrase). Taking this verse as our cue, we can see that we begin our life with God by trusting him or putting our life in his hands. In turn, we do this by speaking to him. The actual words do not matter, but the sentiment needs to be along these lines: "God, I unreservedly surrender my life into your hands." Humbly placing our lives in God's hands enables him to forgive and cleanse us, ready for the future, as well as for a new life with him now.

## Preparing to live

Millions of cruel and selfish lives testify to the possibility of living without regard for our life after death. But Blaise Pascal (1623–62), the French polymath, gives a warning to those of us who are tempted to live without regard for the future. He says, "The present is never our end. The past and the present are our means; the future alone is our end. So we never live, but we hope to live."[2]

The New Testament writers were convinced that the future life we anticipate with God has already invaded the earth and become available to those whose lives are identified with Jesus of Nazareth. The most remarkable good news from the writers of the New Testament is that it is possible for us to begin to enjoy that life now, even if that life will often be overshadowed by creatures and a creation not yet fully aware or affected by the coming of God in Jesus to this planet. The New Testament writers are convinced that it is already possible to live a life that is not characterized by strife, jealousy, anger, quarrels, and envy, for example. Instead, it is their experience that it is possible to live a life that is shot through with love, joy, peace, patience, kindness, generosity, faithfulness, gentleness and self-control (see Galatians 5:16–22). If this is the case, most of us will want to ask: how can we begin to live the life after death in this life?

It is not the case that when we grasp the truth of what we could call the "future certainties", which I listed above, that we are able to ignore our present life, hoping to find in the future the happiness that eludes us in the present. Indeed, when the certainty of the nature of our future becomes part of the way we understand our existence, we are given hope and purpose in this life.

In other words, if we take time to reflect on the expectation that we will continue to live beyond the doorway of our death, into a future that is both profoundly different yet decidedly continuous with the life we have begun to live here, we cannot help but live differently. If, in the future, we are going to be living with God in a spiritual realm or, as C. S. Lewis put it, wither and die without the presence of God, only the most grossly short-sighted of us would not adjust our minds and lives to take this into account.

## Prepare now!

From my reading of the New Testament I would suggest that we prepare to live the life of heaven now, by making sure that we allow God to bring his life to us. If this is our intention our lives will have a number of characteristics.

First, our lives will be characterized by *surrender to God in Jesus*. Matthew quotes Jesus as saying: "those who want to save their life will lose it, and those who lose their life for my sake will find it" (Matthew 16:25). The easiest way to be certain that our lives are surrendered to God is to take time to tell God that we want to surrender our lives to him. Once again, there is no need for any particular words, but the sentiment of our surrender needs to be along the lines of our initial surrender to God: "God, I unreservedly surrender my life into your hands."

Secondly, if we are going to begin heaven on earth, another characteristic of our lives will be *openness to God*. God's life and the life he has for us after we die will be experienced as love, joy, peace, patience, kindness, generosity, faithfulness, gentleness and self-control. If we want to begin that life now, we need to allow God to bring these things to our lives. In this life he does that through filling us and influencing us by his Spirit. Our part in this is – probably as often as we wish! – to ask God to fill us and influence us by his Spirit.

However, we are not mere divine robots. We are free individuals whom God wants to see reach our potential and with whom he wants to have a relationship. Therefore, thirdly, if we are going to experience heaven on earth we need to *cooperate with God* in deciding to take on the life God wants to give us. As we would talk about dressing for the day with clothes prepared for us, Saint Paul talked of "clothing ourselves" or "putting on" what we might call the characteristics of heaven, as much as having them given to us. At one point in writing a letter he says:

Set your minds on things that are above, not on things that are on earth, for you have died, and your life is hidden with Christ in God . . . Put to death, therefore, whatever in you is earthly: fornication, impurity, passion, evil desire, and greed (which is idolatry) . . . As God's chosen ones, holy and beloved, clothe yourselves with compassion, kindness, humility, meekness, and patience . . . Above all, clothe yourselves with love, which binds everything together in perfect harmony (Colossians 3:1–3, 5, 12–14).

One of the "probable certainties" in an uncertain world is that death is not the end. We have seen in this book that a decision to surrender and cooperate with God in this life determines our future beyond the grave. C. S. Lewis said, "Once a man is united to God how could he not live for ever? Once a man is separated from God, what can he do but wither and die?"

## Notes

1 E. Kübler-Ross, "Death Does Not Exist", *Coevolution Quarterly* (Summer, 1977), p. 103, cited in Paul and Linda Badham, *Immortality or Extinction?* (London: Macmillan, 1982), p. 78.

2 Blaise Pascal, *Pensées*, No. 172. ET by W. F. Trotter (Everyman ed.), 1943, pp. 49f. cited in Jürgen Moltmann, *Theology of Hope* (London: SCM, 1967), pp. 26–27.

# Further Reading

## General

Paul and Linda Badham, *Immortality or Extinction?* (London: Macmillan, 1982)
Argues for personal life after death, paying particular attention to paranormal data.

David L. Edwards, *After Death? Past Beliefs and Real Possibilities* (London: SCM, 1999)
Immensely readable and informed discussion, concluding that, unless we refuse the opportunity, "we shall be embraced" by God when we die.

John Hick, *Death and Eternal Life* (Louisville, KY: Westminster/John Knox, 1976, revised 1994)
The classic, wide-ranging discussion, sympathetically informed by non-Christian religions, reaching the conclusion that after we die there will be a period in which the process of our perfecting can continue, perhaps involving reincarnations in other worlds, before we are united in the ultimate oneness of mankind, wholly open to God.

C. S. Rodd, *Is There Life After Death?* (Peterborough, UK: Epworth, 1998)
In an easy-to-read style, the subject is introduced through issues that arise in everyday life, the death of loved ones and a pet, and a near-death experience. Discussion questions follow each chapter.

## 1. Is Death the End?

Paul Badham, *Christian Beliefs About Life After Death* (London: SPCK, 1978)
  Defends the idea of life after death as immortality of the soul, not resurrection. A balanced, wide-ranging, readable treatment.

Stephen T. Davis, ed., *Death and Afterlife* (London: Macmillan, 1989)
  Scholarly essays covering the main issues relating to life after death.

## 2. Where Did it All Start?

Richard N. Longenecker, ed., *Life in the Face of Death: The Resurrection Message of the New Testament* (Grand Rapids, MI and Cambridge, UK: Eerdmans, 1998)
  The book's first section deals with ancient beliefs about life after death in the context of New Testament studies.

James B. Pritchard, *Ancient Near Eastern Texts Relating to the Old Testament* (Princeton: Princeton University Press, 1955)
  Translations of ancient texts, helping set Old Testament beliefs in context.

## 3. Do We Come Back to This Life?

Mark C. Albrecht, *Reincarnation: A Christian Critique of a New Age Doctrine* (Downers Grove: IVP, 1982)
  Written to answer the questions of contemporary readers.

Herman Häring and Johann-Baptist Metz, eds., *Reincarnation or Resurrection?* Concilium (London: SCM and Maryknoll, NY: Orbis, 1993, part 5)
  A collection of essays ranging over different cultures and religions.

## 4. Do We Have an Immortal Soul?

Richard Swinburne, *The Evolution of the Soul* (Oxford: Clarendon, 1997)
A technical argument for the existence of the soul in which the last chapter deals with the future beyond death.

Keith Ward, *The Battle for the Soul* (London: Hodder & Stoughton, 1985)
A careful and accessible defence of the existence of the soul.

## 5. Will We Have Bodies?

Oscar Cullmann, *Immortality of the Soul or Resurrection of the Dead? The Witness of the New Testament* (London: Epworth, 1958)
A small book that argues against the error of immortality.

Murray J. Harris, *Raised Immortal: Resurrection and Immortality in the New Testament* (London: Marshall, Morgan & Scott, 1983)
Argues that the New Testament sees immortality as a consequence of resurrection: "It is only by means of a resurrection transformation that the believer gains immortality."

## 6. Do We Get a Second Chance?

Michael J. Taylor, *Purgatory* (Huntington, IN: Our Sunday Visitor, 1998)
A Roman Catholic examination of the biblical and traditional grounds for belief in purgatory, arguing it to be part of God's plan for us.

Stephen H. Travis, *Christ and the Judgement of God* (Basingstoke: Marshall Pickering, 1986)
A well-informed study of individual passages related to the wider theological issues of life after death.

## 7. Can a Good God Condemn Some of Us to Hell?

William V. Crockett, ed., *Four Views on Hell* (Grand Rapids, MI: Zondervan, 1996)
Full and readable account of the various views on hell which are commonly believed.

David L. Edwards, and John R. W. Stott, *Essentials* (London: Hodder & Stoughton, 1990)
The famous and gracious debate between two British churchmen that includes issues relating to our theme.

## 8. What is Heaven Like?

Colleen McDannell and Bernhard Lang, *Heaven: A History* (New Haven and London: Yale University Press, 1988)
Thorough and always interesting survey of even the most eccentric views.

N. T. Wright, *New Heavens, New Earth: The Biblical Picture of Christian Hope* (Cambridge: Grove, 1999)
A small though helpful book, taking the New Testament seriously.

## 9. How Can We Live if We are Going to Die?

C. S. Lewis, *Mere Christianity* (London: HarperCollins)
The classic introduction to the essence of Christianity.

# Index of Names and Subjects

# Index of Biblical Passages

224